Not Forsaken

Louie Giglio

Finding Freedom as
Sons & Daughters of a Perfect Father

LifeWay Press®
Nashville, Tennessee

Editorial Team

Chris James
Writer

Reid Patton
Content Editor

David Haney
Production Editor

Jon Rodda
Art Director

Joel Polk
Editorial Team Leader

Brian Daniel
Manager, Short-Term Discipleship

Michael Kelley
Director, Discipleship and Groups Ministry

Published by LifeWay Press® • © 2019 Louie Giglio

ISBN 978-1-5359-7016-7 • Item 005817745

Dewey decimal classification: 231.1
Subject headings: FATHER-CHILD RELATIONSHIP / GOD—FATHERHOOD / CHILDREN OF GOD

Unless indicated otherwise, Scripture quotations are taken from the Holy Bible, New International Version®, NIV®. Copyright © 1973, 1978, 1984, 2011 by Biblica, Inc.™ Used by permission of Zondervan. All rights reserved worldwide. www.zondervan.com. The "NIV" and "New International Version" are trademarks registered in the United States Patent and Trademark Office by Biblica, Inc.™ Scripture quotations marked KJV are taken from the Holy Bible, King James Version. Scripture quotations marked ESV are taken from the ESV® Bible (The Holy Bible, English Standard Version®), copyright © 2001 by Crossway, a publishing ministry of Good News Publishers. Used by permission. All rights reserved.

To order additional copies of this resource, write to LifeWay Resources Customer Service; One LifeWay Plaza; Nashville, TN 37234; fax 615-251-5933; call toll free 800-458-2772; order online at LifeWay.com; or email orderentry@lifeway.com.

Printed in the United States of America

Groups Ministry Publishing • LifeWay Resources • One LifeWay Plaza • Nashville, TN 37234

Contents

About the Author

Louie Giglio is the pastor of Passion City Church and the founder of the Passion movement, which exists to call a generation to leverage their lives for the fame of Jesus.

Since 1997 Passion has gathered college-aged young people in events across the United States and around the world. Notably, in 2017 more than fifty-five thousand students gathered for Passion 2017 in Atlanta's Georgia Dome for one of the largest Jesus-focused collegiate events in history. Each year Passion continues to see eighteen- to twenty-five-year-olds fill venues across the nation in pursuit of lives lived for God's glory.

In addition to the collegiate gatherings of Passion Conferences, Louie and his wife, Shelley, lead the teams at Passion City Church, sixstepsrecords, and the Passion Global Institute.

Louie is the author of national best sellers *Not Forsaken* and *Goliath Must Fall; The Comeback; The Air I Breathe; I Am Not but I Know I Am;* and *Indescribable: 100 Devotions about God and Science,* his first children's book.

Louie and Shelley make their home in Atlanta, Georgia.

Introduction

This study is for everyone who has a father. And for everyone who knows what it's like to long for a father's blessing—a father's approval, affection, and attention. For anyone who longs to hear your daddy say, "I love you, and I'm so proud of you."

Maybe that blessing has been present in your life. But maybe it hasn't. Or maybe the blessing was there for a time, but then it slipped away. Or maybe the approval was never there in quite the way you wanted it to be. You always felt it was performance-based instead of unconditional.

Many of us have never known the blessing—or the full blessing—of our earthly dads. What's worse, some of us are stuck with the fact that the possibility of ever hearing our dads say, "I love you, and I'm so proud of you" is gone—washed away by death, distance, or disinterest. The blessing we long for is mired in a pit of regret, pain, or abandonment. This is our reality, and we can do little or nothing to change it. We feel it's too late.

Longing for our father's approval is innate and universal, and we definitely didn't always get it from the man who was responsible for bringing us into this world.

We all have different experiences with our dads, but the craving for our fathers' approval is the same. Maybe you fully possess that blessing, and you're thinking, *I love my dad!* That's a gift I hope you'll thank him for today. But maybe there's a palpable, uneasy silence right now as you're reading, and you're thinking about bailing on this study. You don't want to peel back the layers of your heart to examine your relationship with your dad. It's too painful, and the hurts are too recent, too real.

Regardless of what your life's journey looks like, I encourage you to stay with me. Keep reading. Why? Because God is offering you a promise that has the power to change your life forever. The promise is this. No matter what your relationship with your earthly dad is like, you have a perfect Father in heaven who loves you and wants to pour out His blessing on you.

The Universal Craving

Start

Welcome to session one of *Not Forsaken!*

Let's begin by getting to know one another.

Take a few moments to introduce yourselves. Share your name, members of your immediate families, and where you grew up.

Who's your favorite TV dad, and what makes him your favorite?

As we begin our study together, it's important to recognize that we're coming from different places. All of us have different experiences with our earthly dads—some good, some not so good. But what unites us is the need that's woven into our souls—the need to be loved, treasured, noticed, and accepted by our fathers.

Even if we've experienced a breakdown in our relationship with our earthly dads, it doesn't mean we can't experience a miracle recovery in our relationship with God. Even though we may bear wounds inflicted by our earthly dads, God can restore us and raise us up healed and whole.

Have someone read aloud 2 Corinthians 6:16-18. Then watch Louie's message.

Watch

Use these statements to follow along as you watch the video message.

We all are longing for our father's blessing.

In my research into the lives of some 75 high-achieving, clearly independent women, I knew that I would find a powerful connection between them and the first men in their lives. What surprised me was how deep (and surprisingly traditional) the bond is, how powerful it remains throughout their lives, and how resilient it can be—even when a father has caused it grievous harm. ... No matter how successful their careers, how happy their marriages, or how fulfilling their lives, women told me that their happiness passed through a filter of their fathers' reactions. Many told me that they tried to remove the filter and—much to their surprise—failed. We know that fathers play a key role in the development and choices of their daughters. But even for women whose fathers had been neglectful or abusive, I found a hunger for approval. They wanted a warm relationship with men who did not deserve any relationship at all.[1] —Peggy Drexler

Life for most boys and for many grown men then is a frustrating search for the lost father who has not yet offered protection, provision, nurturing, modeling, or, especially, anointment.[2]—Frank Pittman

ANOINTMENT: being chosen, being blessed, or being approved

I will be a Father to you, and you will be my sons and daughters, says the Lord Almighty.
2 CORINTHIANS 6:18

Video sessions available at lifeway.com/notforsaken

Discuss

Use the following questions to discuss Louie's message.

In what way(s) did you identify with Louie's story about his new nickname from his dad? Or how was it difficult for you to identify with his story?

What word best describes your relationship with your earthly father? Why did you choose that word?

On the video Louie said, "We all are longing for our father's blessing. Every one of us is intrinsically wired with a desire for our father's approval, our father's affection, and our father's participation in our lives. We are starving for it."

How have you found these statements to be true in your life?

Read 2 Corinthians 6:18. Do you think it's possible to relate to God as Father, receiving His approval, affection, and blessing in your life? Why or why not?

What stumbling blocks are keeping you from basking in your Heavenly Father's love for you?

Pray

Close the session with prayer. Remember to complete the following personal studies before the next group session.

Personal Study: Day 1

You Have Worth

Human beings crave approval, especially from our dads. That longing is unquestionably present when we're growing up. We crave our dad's attention and approval when we're kids, and we want so badly to hear him say:

- "That was incredible, Baby Girl!"

- "Wow, Ace [that's what my dad called me]! That was the best dive of all time!"

- "I see you, Princess! Do it again!"

- "Way to go, Son! You're getting so much better!"

Yet—and I'm guessing this statement comes as no surprise—that longing is still there when we're older too, even though it may show up in different, more complex ways. Every one of us is desperate for the approval of our father, no matter what our age. Whether we're doing cartwheels in the living room or presenting proposals in the boardroom, we're looking for approval and affirmation from our dads.

What's the most memorable word of affirmation you've ever received?

What are some ways people might try to gain acceptance and approval?

We're all desperate for our fathers' approval. Without it we can feel given up on, abandoned, deserted, or disowned. We can feel ignored, isolated, jilted, or judged. This void, this lack of a father's presence and approval, can feel like a shadow that always lingers around us, an intangible missing piece we don't know how to find. When that approval isn't present, we feel forsaken.

Our relationship with our dad shapes our sense of acceptance and worth. His influence affects us in multiple ways, but let's consider two polar opposites. On the negative end, a lifetime of hurt or absence from Dad can make us feel that we don't matter—that we're unloved, worthless, or alone. On the positive end, a lifetime of blessing and affirmation from Dad might lead us to think we're the center of someone's universe—that we're relationally sufficient. Both ends of the spectrum affect our sense of identity and worth more than we may think. And the reality is that most of us fall somewhere between the two, a fact that further complicates our outlook on our identity, belonging, and sense of worth.

As you think about your life experience with your dad, which end of the spectrum most closely describes that experience?

Negative   Positive   Somewhere in the middle

Take a moment to pause and reflect. How would you describe your sense of acceptance and value?

What or who defines your identity? Explain.

These are important questions to consider. Few convictions are more important for human beings than knowing who we are and what defines us. If we don't get our identity right, confusion, struggle, and pain will follow us through life. So before we dive deeper into our relationship with our dad, let's go to the Bible to understand who God says we are and what ultimately defines our worth.

Image Bearers

READ GENESIS 1:26-27; 5:1-3.

What words are repeated in these verses?

In these two passages from Genesis, the word *image* is found four times, while the word *likeness* is found three more. These two terms serve as a foundation for identifying our ultimate worth. To be made in the image or likeness of God means humanity is like God in ways that the rest of the creation isn't. God made the moon and the planets, but they're not designing shuttles to transport anyone there. The mountains reflect the handiwork of God, but they can't describe it. God created all the animals of the land—even the duck-billed platypus—but they're not expounding on quantum physics. But you and me? We're made in the image of God. That means we're image bearers of the one true God. And we're more like our Heavenly Father than we might think.

What emotions do you experience when you consider the fact that you were made in the image of God?

Nothing on earth defines your ultimate identity or personal worth—not your circumstances, not your education, not your socioeconomic level, not your abilities, not your career, not your sexuality, and not even your parents. That means before you ever knew your parents as Mom and Dad (or even if you never knew them at all), you already had inherent worth because you were made in the image and likeness of God.

What identities do you need to let go of in order to take hold of your God-given identity?

His Offspring

Read Acts 17:26-28. Record words or phrases that illustrate our relationship to God and His relationship to us.

What does it tell you about God that He is near to you and eager to find you?

When addressing the unbelieving crowd at the Areopagus, the apostle Paul said God relates to us in several different ways.

GOD IS OUR CREATOR. "From one man he made all the nations" (v. 26). This means God created all human beings, including you.

GOD IS OUR SOVEREIGN LORD. "He marked out their appointed times in history and the boundaries of their lands" (v. 26). This means God is in ultimate control of everything on earth, including where you were born and raised.

GOD IS OUR SUSTAINER. "In him we live and move and have our being" (v. 28). This means God isn't distant from you. He's literally the source of your life and being at this very moment.

GOD IS OUR FATHER. "We are his offspring" (v. 28). This means God is your Father and you're His son or daughter.

Yes, God demands worship as your Creator and Lord. And yes, He's the very ground of your existence. But don't miss the subtle truth found in verse 28: you're God's offspring, His son or daughter (see 2 Cor. 6:18). God is your Father!

Your worth is fixed because you're an image bearer and the offspring of God. This is good news regardless of your parental circumstances. If you come from a place of blessing and closeness with your dad, a Father exists who's even greater than he. If you come from a place of pain or neglect, the promise of Scripture is this. No matter what the circumstances are with your earthly dad, you have a perfect Father in heaven who loves you and wants to pour out His blessing on you. The Bible says:

Though my father and mother forsake me, the LORD will receive me.
PSALM 27:10

How should you respond to God for being your perfect Heavenly Father?

Prayer

Father, I confess that I've often found my identity and worth in the people and things around me. I marvel at the fact that I'm made in Your image, and I'm thankful that You've said I'm Your child. Give me grace to wrestle with the hard truths I'll encounter as I work through this study.

You Are Known

Meet Brandon. He's a well-liked art major at a state university, where he works hard, makes good grades, and is active in his campus ministry. If you saw him, you'd think he's got it all together and possesses all the blessings a student could ever want. But there's a hidden problem. Brandon comes from a broken home. He never knew his parents as a couple, and he was raised by his grandparents. His childhood years were spent splitting weekends between his mom and his dad. And although no major conflict ever occurred, the relationship between Brandon and his dad has always been distant. He doesn't see his dad more than once a year, and phone calls are sparsely shared. Now a young man entering adulthood, Brandon calls his dad, longing for a deeper relationship. But the conversations never go beyond sports, politics, and the weather. Brandon can't understand why a father wouldn't want to know his son. Introspective and defeated, he muses, *I'm doing so many great things in my life. If only he would get to know me.*

Brandon has grown from being a boy to a man, but he still has a deep longing to be known by his dad, not on the surface level but at the heart level.

Among your family and friends, who knows you best—the real you?

Just as human beings yearn for approval and worth, we also long to be known—and to be deeply known. And when we don't feel that we're known by our parents, we're left feeling isolated or abandoned. Those feelings can then lead to a whole host of responses. We might erect relational walls, refusing to let others in. Or we can go to the other extreme by sharing to a fault without a filter. We were created to know and be known by others, especially our parents.

Indicate on the scale how well you feel that you're known by your dad.

1	2	3	4	5	6	7	8	9	10
Not at all							*Couldn't be better*		

What's one detail you wish your dad knew about you?

What stands out most about the way your dad pursued you?

Maybe you're reading these questions, but you don't have an earthly dad. Perhaps you never knew him, or maybe he's no longer living. That's not an easy station in life for anyone. I don't want to be callous or to ignore real hurt or absence. But I want to help you process your thoughts too. So here's a question for you:

What have you most longed for from a dad?

Some of these questions might be difficult, but don't let the difficulty push you away. Instead, allow them to expose the need in your heart so that you're prepared to receive the answer to that need. We're going to learn today that your longing to be known can be satisfied by God. Whether you have a blessed or an estranged relationship with your dad, you're perfectly known by your Heavenly Father. And it's a deeper knowledge than even the best dad on earth could ever give.

God Knows Everything

Psalm 139 is one of the most personal passages of Scripture in all the Bible. In it we see the depth of God's knowledge of, presence in, and design for our lives. Each way God is involved in our lives is illustrated through a display of who He is.

READ PSALM 139:1-6.

Record the significant details God knows about you.

God is omniscient. Simply put, that means God knows everything—including everything about you! He knows your actions, your ways, your comings and goings, and even all of your words—before they're audibly spoken. Your Heavenly Father knows your deepest thoughts, highest aspirations, and wildest dreams. He's intimately acquainted with all of your victories, struggles, fears, and doubts. The psalmist David was overwhelmed in response to God's deep, personal knowledge of his life.

Why is it good that God knows us personally, truly, and deeply?

God Is Present Everywhere

God isn't defined by space and time. He's literally present everywhere. That means God is omnipresent. He not only knows everything about you, but He's also with you wherever you go.

READ PSALM 139:7-12.

Many of us know what it means for our dad to have missed an important event or to have been at work when we needed him most. Some people experience these absences as isolated events in the midst of an otherwise blessed existence. Others know these as the norm. The psalmist David proclaimed the good news that your Heavenly Father never misses an important date. He never fails to show up. And He will never leave you or forsake you (see Heb. 13:5).

According to Psalm 139:7-12, why should it comfort you to know that God is always with you?

God Is All-Powerful

In addition to being all-knowing and ever-present, God is all-powerful. He's omnipotent. You can see His power on full display in the next section of Psalm 139, illustrated in the intricate ways He created you.

READ PSALM 139:13-16.

Reflect on the way God intricately and personally designed your body and your life. Record any words or phrases from these verses that you find especially meaningful.

You may have inherited your grandfather's nose or your mother's laugh, but your Heavenly Father ultimately designed, created, and gave the gift of life to you. This means no one knows you like your Creator. No matter the joys or sorrows you've experienced with your earthly father, your Heavenly Father knows you, accompanies you, and fashions you as no other father can.

Precious Promise

Next David reflected on the continual, vast thoughts of God toward His children.

READ PSALM 139:17-18.

Here's the liberating truth to grasp and hold on to as you go through life: your Heavenly Father knows you. He's with you always. And He will never abandon you or let you down. Just as you're known by God, He also wants to be known. Jesus said knowing God is the ultimate meaning of life:

> This is eternal life: that they know
> you, the only true God, and Jesus
> Christ, whom you have sent.
>
> JOHN 17:3

Simply going to heaven when we die isn't the goal of the Christian life. Jesus tells us that the ultimate end to which all of existence points is for us to know God. All of your life—from the time you give your life to Jesus and continuing throughout eternity—should be characterized by a deepening knowledge of and love for your Heavenly Father.

Prayer

Father, You're all-knowing, all-powerful, and present everywhere. I marvel at Your works, and I'm humbled by the vast sum of Your precious thoughts toward me. Give me grace to be satisfied by Your presence in my life now and forever.

You Have Meaning

Why am I here? This is quite possibly the most important question a human being could ever ask. Because God has uniquely and personally created each of us, human life demands value, meaning, and purpose. We're all looking for meaning in one form or another. And Americans usually identify family as the primary place in which we find meaning and purpose.

In a survey conducted by Pew Research Center, almost 70 percent of American adults identified the family as the central place where meaning is found. That's 3½ times more than the number who listed spirituality and faith.[3] We can't disregard the degree to which our family affects our sense of meaning and purpose.

What are some other areas in which people might look to find meaning and purpose in life?

You Aren't an Accident

This week you've already seen that God intentionally and personally created you. These truths present an important principle you should never forget: you aren't an accident. Regardless of the circumstances surrounding your conception, God planned to create you. And what He planned in His mind, He brought to fruition with His creative hands. Whether you and your parents are close or even if you don't know one or both of them at all, you aren't an accident. If you're alive on planet Earth right now, it's because your Heavenly Father wanted you to be here.

What happens in our hearts and souls when we see ourselves as being an accident? What shifts when we begin to grasp that God made each of us with purpose?

Family is an amazing gift from God. And like all gifts, we should receive our families with hearts of gratitude. But we should never enjoy the gifts more than the Giver. We should never place any gift from God on a higher pedestal than God Himself. Even though our families can be a great source of enjoyment and encouragement, they should never be our source of ultimate fulfillment or purpose. Then where do you find them? Why are you here? That's where God comes in.

Ultimate Meaning in Life

READ ISAIAH 43:6-7.

What words did God use in these verses to refer to His people?

According to these verses, what's the purpose for which God creates us?

God says He creates all of His sons and daughters for His glory. That word *all* includes you. God has wired each of us with unique abilities, aptitudes, and desires. Our reason for being is to know and love our Maker and to enjoy Him forever. Nothing is more important than that core purpose. Yet within our relationship with God, He tailors us to make unique contributions to His work in the world, giving our individual lives very specific meaning and direction.

You may come from a healthy, loving family, but without a relationship with your Heavenly Father, you'll miss the purpose of your life. The converse is also true. Even if you suffer from dysfunction, abuse, or loss in your family, you can still experience ultimate meaning in life. It's available to all through God's perfect Son, Jesus Christ.

READ ROMANS 3:23.

How does sin keep us from living out the purpose for which God created us?

Read Jesus' words in John 17:4. What makes Jesus completely different from us?

How does entering a life-changing relationship with Jesus allow us to honor and glorify God the way we're designed to?

God created us with worth and purpose, but sin thwarts our purpose and distorts our understanding of ourselves. Because of sin, none of us glorify God the way He intended. We were all created for God's glory, but we all fall short of it. That means by ourselves we can't fulfill the reason for which God created us. Jesus came to earth to live the perfect life we were required to live and die the punishing death we were required to die in order to make a way for us to fulfill God's purpose for our lives. While we fall short of the glory of God, Jesus perfectly glorified God on earth. Jesus is the means for us to experience ultimate meaning in life.

So What Now?

No one is born into the family of God. Adoption into His family comes through His Son, Jesus. In His own words Jesus tells us how we can enter God's family:

> "The time has come," he said.
> "The kingdom of God has come near.
> Repent and believe the good news!"
> MARK 1:15

Jesus summed up the good news of how to be adopted into God's family with two requirements.

1. Turn away from your sin. This means confessing to God that you're a sinner who fails to glorify Him with your life. It also means turning away from your life of sin (repenting) and starting to walk in obedience to God.

2. Trust in Jesus Christ, believing by faith that He lived the perfect life you were required to live and died the death you were required to die. Believe that just as He rose from the grave on the third day, He will give eternal life to all who place their faith in Him.

Can you point to a time in your life when you were adopted into the family of God through repentance and faith? If so, when?

If not, do you want to be adopted now? If so, pray to your Heavenly Father, confess your sin, and ask Jesus to save you or reach out to a trusted friend or pastor to help you act on that decision.

When you place your faith in Jesus, God adopts you into a new family with a new purpose and meaning. The Bible says:

> ## To all who did receive him [Jesus], to those who believed in his name, he gave the right to become children of God.
> JOHN 1:12

Once you understand who gives you worth, who knows you, and who defines your purpose, you can take your first steps to receive your Heavenly Father's blessing and to confront any regrets over your relationship with your earthly father.

Prayer

Father, thank You for creating me with purpose and for adopting me into Your eternal family through Your Son, Jesus. Please open my heart to believe the truths of Your Word as I continue this study.

---

1. Peggy Drexler, "Daughters and Dad's Approval," *Psychology Today,* June 27, 2011, https://www.psychologytoday.com/us/blog/our-gender-ourselves/201106/daughters-and-dads-approval.
2. Frank Pittman, "Fathers and Sons," *Psychology Today,* September 1, 1993, https://www.psychologytoday.com/us/articles/199309/fathers-and-sons.
3. "Where Americans Find Meaning in Life," Pew Research Center, November 20, 2018, https://www.pewforum.org/2018/11/20/where-americans-find-meaning-in-life/.

Reflect

What did you learn from this week's study that you didn't know before?

In what sources other than God are you tempted to find ultimate meaning in life?

If someone asked you, "What defines your identity, value, and worth?" how would you respond after completing this week's study?

Connect

In this study we're going to tackle some deep truths and challenging issues. Dealing with challenges is best done with others. Make a commitment to faithfully attend each group session and to complete all of the personal studies.

Reach out to a fellow group member and ask how you can specifically pray for him or her in the coming week.

Record a prayer for fellow group members in the space provided.

The Most Important Thing about You

Start

Welcome to session two!

To get started this week, let's share a quick memory. What was your most anticipated Christmas gift as a child?

Last week we talked about our universal craving for a father's blessing. We learned that regardless of where circumstances stand with our earthly father, we can still experience a miracle recovery in our relationship with our Heavenly Father.

Review your notes in last week's Reflect section. What truths stood out to you most?

How did God challenge you this week?

In session one we addressed some common misunderstandings about our identity and established who we are as children of God. In this session we're going to explore some of our misunderstandings about God and seek to understand who He is as our Heavenly Father.

Have someone read aloud Ephesians 1:17-18. Then watch Louie's message.

Watch

Use these statements to follow along as you watch the video message.

What comes into our minds when we think about God is the most important thing about us.[1] —A. W. Tozer

All of us were created to move toward God.

When we think about God, it's essential that we think about Him in the right way.

What Jesus teaches us most about God is that He is a Father.

God doesn't want us to know Him officially. God wants us to know Him intimately.

Discuss

Use the following questions to discuss Louie's message.

A. W. Tozer said, "What comes into our minds when we think about God is the most important thing about us."[2] What comes into your mind when you think about God?

How does our idea of God shape the rest of our thought life?

On the video Louie talked about some distorted views of God. Which of these distorted views have you gravitated toward?

Grandpa God   Scorekeeper God   Concierge (Alexa) God

Lightning-bolt God   No God

How has God corrected those views over time? In what ways do those distorted views still show up in your life?

Were you surprised to learn that Jesus talked about God as Father more than any other title? Why or why not? Why is this significant?

Louie said, "God doesn't want us to know Him officially. God wants us to know Him intimately. God's not inviting you into a handshake relationship. He's inviting you into an embrace—the loving embrace of a perfect Heavenly Father."

What's the difference between knowing God officially and knowing Him intimately? Why is this distinction important?

Pray

Close the session with prayer. Remember to complete the following personal studies before the next group session.

A Wide View of God

What do you imagine God is like? On what have you based your idea of God?

Everybody has an idea of God in mind, and there are a ton of different viewpoints, some helpful, some not so helpful. Your concept of God could have come from a lot of places. Maybe your mom and dad told you at a young age what God was like, and you incorporated a lot of their ideas, some helpful, some not so helpful. Likely the culture and the part of the world you grew up in played a big part in shaping your image of God. Regardless of the sources of influence, A. W. Tozer reminds us that "we tend by a secret law of the soul to move toward our mental image of God."[3]

Which of the following played the greatest role in shaping your viewpoint about God?

___ *Parents*   ___ *Church*   ___ *Friends*

___ *Life experiences*   ___ *Media*   ___ *Other:* _____

This may surprise you, but God wants you to know who He is. He's not hiding like a needle in a haystack, saying, "Good luck figuring out who I really am." He's not plunking you down in a spiritual corn maze, some kind of twisted game with eternal stakes. On the contrary, God has surrounded you with His own fingerprints on His creation and has overcome every possible hurdle to show you who He is and what He's like. More than you want to find God, God wants you to find Him. He wants you to know Him and to know how much He loves you.

God Can Be Known

Believe it or not, God is very knowable. He constantly shows us who He is. God knows the stakes are high because if we don't know who He truly is, we could spend our whole lives with the wrong idea of Him in mind, living our days on earth trying to respond to a flawed image of Him. Because we were designed to know God, our idea of God inevitably shapes our idea of ourselves.

How does a wrong view of God keep us from experiencing the blessing of knowing God?

Thankfully, we don't have to wonder what God is like. God has revealed Himself to us. He hasn't left us in the dark. God shows us who He is and what He's like in three primary ways. Each of these is integral in forming as comprehensive a view of God as possible.

1. God reveals Himself through what He made—the creation.

2. God reveals Himself through what He wrote—the Bible.

3. God reveals Himself through the One He sent—His Son, Jesus.

Today we'll examine the first way God reveals Himself to humanity: through creation.

Read the following Scriptures and record any words or phrases that point to God's activity in creation.

Genesis 1:1

Psalm 33:6

Psalm 90:2

John 1:1-3

Acts 17:24-25

Colossians 1:16

Each of these verses points to the fact that God created the heavens, the earth, and everything in them. He's the power and creative genius behind everything we see and enjoy in the universe. Furthermore, the psalmist tells us:

> ## Before the mountains were born or you brought forth the whole world, from everlasting to everlasting you are God.
> PSALM 90:2

This verse affirms that God created the world *ex nihilo*, which means "out of nothing." Only God can create something from nothing.

How can these verses and truths affect the way you view creation the next time you walk out your door?

"God created the heavens and the earth" (Gen 1:1). Although that's a powerful truth, it tells us only the what and not the why. Stay with me because this is where we'll start seeing the connection between creation and our ability to know God.

READ PSALM 19:1-2 AND ROMANS 1:19-20.

A common reason people claim not to believe in God is the supposed lack of evidence for God. How would you respond to this objection, based on the two previous passages?

According to these two passages, anybody anywhere on planet Earth can look around and consider the universe—the mountains and waterfalls, the animals and sunsets, the stars and volcanoes, the marvelous flight-producing design of a feathered bird, the half billion neurons in the motor cortex of your brain that enable you to talk— and conclude that a divine Being must be behind it all.

That's good news. Nature shows us there's a God—a creative, beautiful, intelligent God. And we can see evidence of God, like perfect fingerprints, all around us. Thanks to all of this created evidence, "people are without excuse" (Rom. 1:20) for not knowing Him.

Where do you most clearly see God's handiwork in the world?

Insufficient Knowledge

Here's what we've learned today. You're wired to know God, and God is, in fact, knowable. He reveals Himself to every man, woman, and child on earth through the beauty and power of what He made. The created world is sufficient evidence to tell you that an intelligent, powerful God is behind it all.

This knowledge of God is a general, or wide, knowledge. In other words, creation provides enough information to know that God exists, but it's insufficient to know what He desires for us. We need more revelation to understand how to relate to our Heavenly Father. We'll start there in tomorrow's study.

How has today's study changed your view of God?

Prayer

Father, I want to declare Your glory and proclaim Your handiwork like the stars and planets. If what I think about You is the most important thing about me, help me understand and know You more as I continue to study.

Personal Study: Day 2

A Deeper View of God

Think for a moment about your favorite actor. You've probably seen all of their movies or shows. Perhaps you follow them on social media, and you might catch some of their interviews. Their movies and interviews show you dimensions of who they are, but media can never allow you to truly know the real person. No matter how often you watch displays of their skill on a screen, you'll never know the depth of their heart without repeated personal encounters.

The same is true about God. Though He showcases His existence, intelligence, and power to every person on earth through what He has made, the creation is insufficient to mine the depths of His heart, the intricacies of His character, and His desires for your life.

Besides leaving clues all over His creation, God gets even more specific in telling us what He's like. Today we'll explore the second way God reveals Himself to His children. He reveals Himself through what He wrote—the Bible. Creation gives us a wide, or general, understanding of who God is, while the Bible gives us a deeper, or more specific, understanding of who He is.

When do you first remember reading the Bible?

What would you say was God's primary purpose in authoring the Bible?

More than a Book

Some people view the Bible as simply another religious book. They approach it like a novel or a work of history. But this isn't the best way to approach the Bible. You see, the Bible isn't really a book as much as it is an anthology. It's actually a collection of sixty-six books. Within that collection you'll find history books, poetry books, prophetic books (written by Old Testament prophets), Gospels (spiritual biographies of Jesus), and Epistles (shorter books consisting of letters written to New Testament churches by the early church leaders). Each type of literature in the Bible is equally Scripture, communicating important aspects of who God is and what He wants for your life.

READ 2 TIMOTHY 3:16.

According to this verse, what's the Bible useful for?

What does it mean for Scripture to be inspired by God?

What makes the Bible different from any other book is that all the words of Scripture are inspired, or breathed out, by God. That means from beginning to end, the words in the Bible are the exact words God intended for us to have. He preserved each verse to teach us who He is, show us His character, and lead us to know Him deeply. The Bible exists to communicate who God is and what He's like.

What changes about your experience reading Scripture when you begin to view it as a personal encounter with God?

How is this view different from what you've thought about the Bible before?

Consider the Book of Psalms in the Old Testament. Psalms is a collection of poems characterized by emotional transparency in praying to and worshiping God. Psalm 119 is the longest chapter in the entire Bible. These 176 verses are all about God's Word. The psalmist used seven different synonyms for God's Word in this chapter: *law, testimonies, precepts, statutes, commandments, rules,* and *Word.* Here are a few benefits of God's Word that the psalmist identified.

- God's Word leads you to worship God (see v. 7).

- God's Word keeps you from sinning against God (see v. 11).

- God's Word teaches you what God has done (see v. 27).

- God's Word comforts you when you're afflicted (see vv. 49-50).

- God's Word tells you what God has promised (see v. 58).

Ultimately, the Bible reveals God to us. And it's a much deeper revelation than what's seen through creation. Each time you read the Scriptures, you experience a real and personal encounter with the Creator of the universe. It's where you learn what He has done, what He's like, what He cares about, what He has promised, and what He desires for your life. God has spoken to us through what has been written in Scripture. God's Word is a trustworthy source through which you can know God.

Why do we need the Bible to know God and to know ourselves?

What is one key truth you've learned from Scripture about God or about yourself?

Going Deeper

Because the Bible is the source for discovering who God is, what He's like, and what He desires for your life, let's get a clearer view of God as revealed in Scripture by learning some of His titles and attributes.

Ruler of the universe	*God of justice*	*The Word that became flesh*
Immortal	*Redeemer*	*Holy*
Mighty Warrior	*Merciful God*	*Love*

Read each of the following verses. Then record the previous attributes of God beside the verses that describe those characteristics.

1 Chronicles 29:11

Isaiah 6:3

Psalm 96:10

Malachi 3:6

Matthew 5:48

Colossians 2:3

1 Peter 1:3

2 Peter 3:9

1 John 1:9

1 John 4:7-8

Which attribute or title of God is most meaningful to you right now? Why?

Which of the previous qualities of God would you like to share with someone else?

God reveals Himself through the pages of the Bible in much more specific ways than the general way we see Him in creation. In His Word we come face-to-face with the person of God. But believe it or not, there's an even more specific, personal way through which God has revealed Himself to us. We'll explore that means of revelation in our next personal study.

Prayer

Use the list of attributes you examined today to thank God for all of the ways He relates to you. Ask Him to meet any specific needs you have.

Personal Study: Day 3

An Intimate View of God

Yesterday we learned that in the Bible, God reveals Himself to us in a specific, personal way. Through the Scriptures we saw several different titles, attributes, and desires of God.

God isn't primarily one particular attribute. He's all of the characteristics and roles we see in Scripture. Yet when Jesus was on earth, He emphasized one quality of God more than any other. He repeated it over and over, driving this characteristic into the souls of His listeners. The number one image of God that Jesus highlighted again and again is this: God is a Father.

Why is the way Jesus primarily identified God significant?

Jesus showed us that God is powerful, majestic, glorious, and full of wisdom and grace and truth, but He's wrapped in the skin of a Father. Many of God's attributes are difficult for us to grasp, but we can embrace a Father who's full of grace and truth. God is relatable. He's knowable. He's forgiving. He's compassionate. He's touchable. The fatherhood of God is the skin that holds together all of His other attributes.

Like Father, like Son

Now we come to the third primary way God reveals Himself to us, and it's the most intimate revelation of them all. God reveals Himself through His Son, Jesus.

Read the following passages and identify the ways Jesus reveals God to us in the flesh.

John 10:30

John 14:8-11

2 Corinthians 4:6

Hebrews 1:1-3

The writer to the Hebrews tells us that the prophets of the Old Testament revealed God in a more specific way than even creation reveals Him. The prophets ultimately pointed people to a coming Messiah, Jesus Christ. Look at verse 3 more closely:

The Son is the radiance of God's glory and the exact representation of his being.
HEBREWS 1:3

The best way to know God is to know Jesus—a walking, talking, living, breathing picture of God on earth. Throughout His ministry Jesus equated Himself with the Father. He told His opponents (see John 10:30) and His close companions (see 14:8-11) that when they looked at Him, they were looking at God in the flesh. Jesus sketched a picture of who God is for all of us to see and understand.

Why do you think Jesus' claims to be God were so difficult for the people He interacted with during His earthly ministry?

READ MATTHEW 3:13-17.

How did God describe Jesus in this moment? Why is His description significant?

The account of Jesus' baptism is one of the first places in Scripture where the fatherhood of God is displayed. Scripture says when Jesus came up out of the water, the heavens opened; the Holy Spirit descended like a dove and alighted on Jesus; and a voice from heaven issued a startling, wonderful announcement. The Father called out, in effect, "This is my Son. I love Him. And I'm really pleased with Him."

We need to meditate on that scene, to soak in its significance. We need to bask in it and enjoy it. Beside the Jordan River that day, God the Father showed that His relationship with Jesus was a deep connection. A family connection. A real, heart-to-heart life connection through which the Creator of the universe acknowledged and blessed His Son.

God is a loving Father. We clearly see this fact as God the Father pulled back the curtain and showed us this amazing relationship with the Son, whom He dearly loved. And God extends a similar relationship to us, a relationship in which He's our Father and we're His sons and daughters. God loves us, and He's proud to call us His own. Let that fact sink in.

How does it make you feel that through Jesus, God extends the same affirmation and love to you?

You Too Can Call Him Father

Through both His relationship with His Father and His teaching, Jesus wants you to see God in a new way: you can know Him as Father. Don't take my word for it. Listen to the words of Jesus. We find this understanding again and again in His teachings. In fact, 189 times in the four Gospels alone, Jesus referred to God as a Father—far more than any other term, role, or characteristic Jesus used to describe Him. Here are just a few examples.

- When Jesus taught why we do good works (see Matt. 5:16)

- When Jesus taught how to pray (see Matt. 6:9)

- When Jesus breathed His last breath (Luke 23:46)

- When Jesus taught how to come to Him for salvation (see John 6:44)

We come to know, embrace, and relate to the Almighty One by approaching Him as our Heavenly Father.

At the end of last week's study, we learned that Jesus, God's perfect Son, gives you the right to become a child of God (see John 1:12). This relationship becomes yours when you trust in God through Jesus Christ. God brings your heart to life, and you're born anew as a son or a daughter of a perfect Heavenly Father. This spiritual birth not only brings us life on the inside but also places us in a new family with a new Father.

READ ROMANS 8:13-17 AND GALATIANS 4:4-7.

Record the main ideas of these passages in your own words.

The New Testament says God is our Abba. The word is Aramaic, the common language of Jesus' day. It was the word kids used when addressing their earthly dads. Abba isn't perfectly translated into English as Daddy or Papa, but it's close to that, a word that's tender, affectionate, and easy for a child to say. The word connotes confidence in a father. It's not a formal title. It's a familiar title. It's what children say when they know they're close to their father and their father is close to them.

God isn't a nebulous force that's impossible to know or understand. He's not your great cosmic butler in the sky. He doesn't live in a stained-glass cathedral, He isn't keeping score on you, and He's not merely your buddy. He's not a bully or a grandpa or the face you look at in the mirror. God is a Father. Through Jesus Christ, God can be your Abba.

How can you live in a way that displays the gratitude and affection you have for your Heavenly Father?

Prayer

Father, thank You for the privilege of calling You Father. Help me depend on You and love You the way a child loves his father.

1. A. W. Tozer, *The Knowledge of the Holy* (New York: HarperOne, 1961), 1.
2. Ibid.
3. Ibid.

Reflect

God reveals Himself to us in three primary ways. What are they?

1.

2.

3.

What you think about God is the most important thing about you. How have your thoughts about God changed as a result of this week's study?

What's the most significant truth you read in Scripture this week?

Connect

This week connect with God by intentionally praising Him and thanking Him for His power displayed through nature. When you see a beautiful sunset, a flowing river, a majestic mountain, or a bee landing on a flower, praise God for His creative genius.

This week connect with others by intentionally sharing a truth from God's Word that you learned in your study.

Seeing God as a Perfect Father

Start

Welcome to session three!

Think about a time when you were at a musical performance, a sporting event, or a scenic overlook and someone or something significantly obstructed your view. Share those experiences with your group. Why are those experiences so frustrating?

Let's review what we've learned so far.

In session one we learned that we all long for our father's blessing. Every one of us is intrinsically wired with a desire for our father's approval, our father's affection, and our father's participation in our lives. Last week we learned that God is indeed knowable. He has revealed Himself to us in three primary ways.

What are the three primary ways God reveals Himself to us?

In last week's personal studies we read several Scriptures and learned numerous truths about who God is. What's the most impactful truth you learned in the personal studies?

Discovering that God wants us to know Him as a perfect Father is only half of the journey. Each of us has a picture of what a father is like, primarily based on our relationship with our earthly dad. Today we're going to go deeper into our personal stories to identify ways our view of God can be distorted by a flawed understanding of what a father is.

Have someone read aloud Matthew 7:11. Then watch Louie's message.

Watch

Use these statements to follow along as you watch the video message.

God is not the reflection of your earthly father; He is the perfection of your earthly father.

Our Father in heaven is the Dad who showed up, who cared enough, who showed us powerfully and spoke to us powerfully His love for us.

Though my father and mother forsake me, the LORD will receive me.
PSALM 27:10

God restores what has been lost.

One in four children in America are living without a father present in their lives.

You can live knowing that you are a loved son, a loved daughter of a perfect Father all the days of your life.

Discuss

Use the following questions to discuss Louie's message.

In what way did you immediately identify with Louie's story about being at the pool as a child? In what way did you have difficulty identifying with his testimony?

On the video Louie said, "God's not just a bigger version of your dad; God is the perfect version of your dad. God is not the reflection of your earthly father; He is the perfection of your earthly father."

If you come from a great relationship with your dad, what's your reaction to the previous quotation? What about for those of you who don't have a great relationship with your dad?

How has your relationship with your dad influenced your view of your Heavenly Father, whether positively or negatively?

Read Psalm 27:10; 68:5-6; and Matthew 7:11. Which words are meaningful to you?

On the video Louie said, "God restores what has been stolen from our lives and even gives a better Father's blessing."

What steps could you take to move out of the paralysis of the past to embrace your Heavenly Father's love for you?

Pray

Close the session with prayer. Remember to complete the following personal studies before the next group session.

Dealing with the Earthly

One of the benefits Shelley and I were looking forward to most when moving from the suburbs to the city was the panoramic view of the downtown skyline we would enjoy from the rooftop of our new townhouse. Granted, we had to climb the utility stairs and take some risks to get to the roof, but those obstacles didn't dampen our enthusiasm in the slightest. We had a stunning city view. That is, until the vacant lot next door became the home to a condominium building eleven feet taller than our rooftop. Eleven feet! Just enough to completely obstruct our skyline vista.

In the same way, your earthly dad may be responsible for erecting an image that's impeding your view of fatherhood. Although God's heart is good and His arms are strong, it's hard for you to see these truths because your earthly dad built a wall just tall enough to block your view.

Let's face it. There's a fatherhood crisis in our world. According to the U.S. Census Bureau, more than one in four children lives in a home without a father.[1] And this fact shouldn't surprise us. The enemy seeks to destroy fatherhood. He wants to break apart our image of what a good father is. He wants to destroy families and wreck the relationships between fathers and their kids. If he can shatter our picture of good earthly fathers, he might in turn distort our image of our perfect Heavenly Father. And if the enemy can't completely shatter our image of God, he might be able to damage it enough to keep us from living fully free in our Heavenly Father's care and blessing.

READ JOHN 10:10.

How could the enemy use your doubts and hurts to obstruct your view of your Heavenly Father?

Six Fathers

I don't pretend to know or fully understand what your dad was or is like, but six father types seem to dominate our stories. Maybe your dad is like one of the following.

1. **THE ABSENT FATHER.** This father could be absent due to death, divorce, distance, or disinterest. The bottom line: he's not present in your life.

2. **THE ABUSIVE FATHER.** This father hurt you emotionally, verbally, physically, sexually, or spiritually. Whatever form the abuse took, you were always wondering where you stood, and maybe you grew up depressed, anxious, defensive, angry, and even suicidal.

3. **THE PASSIVE FATHER.** He might be a nice guy, but this father is weak and mostly silent. He refused to take up the mantle of leadership and proved to have little positive influence in your life and family.

4. **THE PERFORMANCE-BASED FATHER.** Life with this dad was always a grind. His blessing and love came with conditions. Only if you acted a certain way, achieved a certain position, or measured up a certain way could you receive his approval.

5. **THE ANTAGONISTIC FATHER.** This dad points out all of your flaws and sows seeds of failure in your mind every time you try something new. He's not for you. He's against you. And before you can succeed in the world, you have to fight your way out of your own home.

6. **THE EMPOWERING FATHER.** This Father is a kind, strong, encouraging dad. He constantly does his best to love his family. He always tells his kids he loves them and makes every attempt to be present for them.

Which of the previous fathers most accurately describes your earthly dad?

If applicable, what specific things has your earthly dad done to distort your view of your Heavenly Father?

If applicable, what specific things has your earthly dad done to enhance your view of your Heavenly Father?

If you've lived with an empowering father, you most likely have a head start on people who didn't. If you've lived with one of the other dads or with a hybrid of a few of them, you may feel that you're still stuck with a twisted view of father that makes it difficult to embrace the idea that God wants you to know Him as Abba Father.

The Origin of Regret

The reality is that we all have pain when we think about our dads—even those of us who have the best dads. And although our circumstances may be unique and complex, the reason for our regrets is simple: no dad is perfect. In fact, the reason goes even deeper than that. It's not just that no dad is perfect. It's that every dad is a sinner. (Every mom, son, and daughter is too.) Sin doesn't involve just making some bad choices. Sin also deeply affects our families, hurts our relationships, and distorts our view of God.

Read the following verses, taking note of humanity's spiritual condition.

Psalm 14:2-3

Psalm 51:5

Ecclesiastes 7:20

Romans 3:23

What clear message does the Bible communicate through these verses?

The Bible talks extensively about the sinfulness of humanity. The previous verses show us this important truth: we're not sinners because we do bad things; we do bad things because we're sinners. This truth is crucial to understand as you think about the regrets and pain you might have experienced because of your dad. I can't tell you why he did what he did. I can't explain to you all of the reasons behind each of your experiences or why your life looks very different from your neighbor's. But I can tell you the source behind it all. The origin of your regrets is sin. Sin has broken the world, has broken our relationships with others, and has distorted our view of God. Dads disappoint us because they're sinners. They break our hearts because they're broken individuals, some more than others. But all dads fall short of the goodness of God.

How does knowing your dad is a sinner affect the way you approach your regrets with him?

Beyond your relationship with your earthly father, how does knowing that we're all sinners help you extend grace and mercy to others?

In order to deal with your past or present hurts from your dad, it's crucial to know the source of that pain. It's also helpful to know that a real enemy exploits those hurts in order to steal, kill, and destroy you and your important relationships. But it's just as crucial to hope in the truth that God wants to restore you. And He wants to give you a life of abundant goodness through His Son, Jesus Christ, who has said:

> ## The thief comes only to steal and kill and destroy; I have come that they may have life, and have it to the full.
>
> JOHN 10:10

That's the good news of the gospel. If God can take you from spiritual death to spiritual life through the death, burial, and resurrection of His Son, Jesus, He can restore every relational deficit in your life.

Prayer

Heavenly Father, I want to have a life of abundant goodness. Please restore the relational deficits I've experienced from my earthly parents. Help me trust that Your heart is good and Your arms are strong.

Embracing the Heavenly

How do you move forward if your trust in the one who should have been the most trustworthy person in your life—your earthly dad—has been damaged, corrupted, or blurred? How can you celebrate the fact that there's a God in heaven who wants you to know him as Abba? If God is a father like yours, why would you want anything to do with Him?

At this point it's good to remember that God isn't the reflection of your earthly dad; He's the perfection of your earthly dad. God isn't just a bigger version of your earthly father; He's everything you've ever wanted your dad to be and much, much more.

What emotion best describes your response to the previous paragraph?

The fact that God is much more than anything you've ever wanted your dad to be is incredibly good news for you. Even if your dad is a wonderful father, you should want a God who's somewhat like him but infinitely better. And if your dad left a wake of pain and confusion, you can still imagine what life would have been like if circumstances had been different.

Maybe you've imagined what life would be like with a loving, engaged, encouraging, interested dad. Have you imagined what his embrace would have felt like? Did you wonder how life would have been different if he had showed up, sobered up, stayed true, and defended you? Have you tried to imagine your dad being like this?

What one blessing do you wish you could receive from a father that you aren't receiving?

What did your dad do for you that you're most thankful for?

If God is the perfect Father, what do you most want to receive from Him?

The good news is that God is what you've imagined all these years. You can use those longings and desires to find your way to Him, knowing He's not an oversized version of your imperfect dad. Rather, he's the Father you've always dreamed of having.

Relating to the Perfect Father

Just as the Bible shows us more clearly who God is, it also informs us more deeply how God relates to us, His children. From the Old Testament to the New Testament, we see that God is an intimately personal, loving, and nurturing Father to us.

Read the following Scriptures and fill in the blanks.

God wants to _____ me (see Ps. 23:4).

God wants to _____ me (see Ps. 59:1).

God wants to _____ me (see Ps. 139:1).

God wants to _____ over me (see Zeph. 3:17).

God wants to _____ me (see Matt. 1:21).

God wants to _____ me (see Heb. 12:6).

God wants to _____ to me (see Jas. 1:17).

God wants to _____ me (see I John 4:7-8).

Consider the previous truths. Which are most meaningful to you now?

Which of the previous truths are most difficult to believe now?

Following the Perfect Example

Is it still difficult to imagine what a relationship with your Heavenly Father could be like? We don't have to imagine it. We can actually see a glimpse of it. We can see it in the way Jesus interacted with the Father during more than thirty years on planet Earth. The four Gospels paint a beautiful picture of the relationship between God the Father and Jesus, His perfect Son. Consider the following realities that characterized the relationship between the Father and the Son.

- The Father loves the Son and is very pleased with Him (see Matt. 3:17).

- The Son depends on the Father for strength and vitality (see Mark 1:35).

- The Son and the Father have enjoyed a relationship for eternity (see John 1:1).

- The Father and the Son share a closeness together (see John 1:18).

- The Son follows the Father's example and instruction (see John 5:19).

- The Son and the Father know each other deeply (see John 10:14-15).

- The Son loves the Father and wants to please the Father (see John 14:31).

In what ways do these truths teach us how we can interact with God as our Heavenly Father?

READ JOHN 17:20-23.

The relationship enjoyed between the Father and the Son serves as the perfect model for the way a child and a father relate to each other. Although we don't know everything about the relationship between God and Jesus, what we know is very instructive. John said the way the Father loves the Son is the same way He loves people who come to Him through Jesus. The love shared between God the Father and Jesus, His Son, is shared with you and me. For people who receive the Son by faith, the Father's love flows to them through the Son.

Compose a simple line of gratitude to God for the ways He pursues a relationship with you, His son or daughter.

From the pages of Scripture, you can know God's real and deep affection for you. He saw you long before you saw Him. You're His unique and purposed creation. He has loved you before there was time. He sought you and paid a ransom for you although you could do nothing to deserve it. He never gave up on you. Before God ever asked anything from you, He gave everything to you in the gift of His Son. You matter to God. You have a destiny. You're somebody. You aren't the center of all creation, but you're dearly loved by the One who is. You have a God to call Father. And you have a God who calls you daughter or son.

Your Father in Heaven is a Healer. He can heal all of the wounds your earthly father may have inflicted. He can pick you up and hold you in His care. He can redeem what has been lost and can make all things new again. His arms are strong, His heart is good, and you can trust Him.

Prayer

Father, You're a good Father who gives good gifts to Your children. Keep drawing me to Yourself so that I can draw near You.

A Path to Healing

Have you ever been involved in an accident in which you were hurt in a significant way and needed medical care? Maybe it was a broken leg or a cut on your hand or arm. I remember a time when I was about ten years old. I was honing my carving skills with a Swiss Army knife my dad gave me. Foolishly, I was carving the wood toward my body when the blade slipped and sliced my left hand, right through the patch of skin that forms the webbing between the thumb and the index finger. Blood went everywhere. I ran to tell my mom, who was entertaining houseguests.

"Mom, I hurt my hand real bad."

Her eyes widened. "Why did you do that?" she asked.

"I was carving with my new knife Dad gave me, and it slipped."

"We'll look at it after our company is gone," she said. "And try not to get blood on the carpet."

This was a classic response by my mom. Though dramatic at times, she always under-reacted when I hurt myself. After her friends went home, she surveyed the cut and patched it with bandages and gauze.

Fifty years later the scar on my left hand confirms that the knife wound left a two-inch opening. It was a gash that required stitches, for sure. But instead of an emergency-room visit, we covered it as best we could, and I tried not to move my thumb for a week or so.

Sadly, things didn't improve. Days went by and the bandages were changed, but the wound looked worse and worse, becoming infected and gross. I never got stitches, and my hand eventually healed, but I can tell you that trying to ignore a wound by covering it up isn't the recommended course of action.

The same is true of wounds to our hearts. We can't simply ignore the sting of our dad's wounds, even though we often try.

What are some ways you try to cover up and mask the hurt from your past?

Often we attempt to cover up our hurt by believing that we don't really care what dad thinks or that we don't need him anyway. You can't get past the wounds of your dad by repeatedly insisting that you're not affected by the wounds left by your father. You can't say you don't need your earthly dad's blessing without admitting there's a blessing you're living without.

Are there any wounds you're attempting to cover up? If so, what are they? Be honest with yourself and with God.

Circle any of the following emotions you've experienced in response to the wounds of your past.

Anger   Bitterness   Loneliness   Shame   Indifference   Depression

Sadness   Inferiority   Forgotten   Resentment   Callousness   Anxiety

Insecurity   Untrusting   Caution   Embarrassment   Grief   Hurt

To get past our wounds, we first have to stare them in the face, admit the ways they've made us feel, and acknowledge the truth of our pain. But we can't stay stuck in the pain, always examining our wounds, always asking why. Our wounds will never heal that way. We must shift our focus, understanding that healing comes neither by ignoring our wounds nor by fixating on them.

What's your tendency—ignoring your wounds or fixating on them? Describe an example.

To experience healing, it's imperative to be honest about your hurts. But it's also important to run to the right source for healing. That brings us to another title of our Heavenly Father. He's our Healer.

The Lord, My Healer

Throughout the Old Testament God continually revealed Himself to His people. At each junction in history, he taught His people the expansive nature of His character. Often He did this by revealing a new name by which His people could know Him. After rescuing His people from slavery in Egypt, God contrasted the disease inflicted on the Egyptians with the protection He promised His people:

> If you listen carefully to the LORD
> your God and do what is right in
> his eyes, if you pay attention to his
> commands and keep all his decrees,
> I will not bring on you any of the
> diseases I brought on the Egyptians,
> for I am the LORD, who heals you.
> EXODUS 15:26

God isn't the destroyer of His people. He's the healer of His people. God is Jehovah Rapha, a name that means "the Lord, our Healer."

In multiple places in the Bible, we continue to see a picture of God as our Healer and Restorer—the haven of safety for our wounded souls.

READ PSALM 147:3; PROVERBS 18:10; ISAIAH 53:5; AND MATTHEW 11:28.

Which verse is most beneficial for your heart right now? Why?

Rewrite the verse you chose. Then commit to memorize it this week.

The Path to Healing

In this study you don't merely want to see facts about who God is or what He wants to do for you. You ultimately want to see a Heavenly Father whose heart is good and whose arms are strong—a Father who's worthy of your trust and embrace. And as you embrace Him, you can start walking down the path to healing we've begun exploring this week and will continue to explore next week.

Based on the four verses we read in the previous activity, we can identify a fourfold process to start walking the pathway to healing.

1. **RECOGNIZE.** Recognize that God is your ultimate Healer, the One who heals the brokenhearted and binds up your wounds (see Ps. 147:3).

2. **RUN.** Run to your Heavenly Father, the One who's a safe refuge for His children (see Prov. 18:10).

3. **REST.** Rest in the arms of your Heavenly Father, the One who doesn't weigh you down but gives rest to your wounded soul (see Matt. 11:28).

4. **REDEEM.** Jesus came not only to pay the price for all of your sins but also to redeem all of your hurts (see Isa. 53:5).

The path to healing is found in focusing on Jesus' wounds:

He was pierced for our transgressions,
he was crushed for our iniquities;
the punishment that brought us
peace was on him,
and by his wounds we are healed.

ISAIAH 53:5

To delve deeper and deeper into your past without a firm grasp of the cross and the victory Jesus won for you there is like trying to escape from handcuffs while you're sinking in quicksand. Wounds are real, and ignoring them can be fatal. But healing is available in the person of Jesus.

What's one step you need to take toward healing this week?

Prayer

Father thank You for exposing my
wounds and for providing healing.
Please give my heart the kind of rest
and relief that only You can provide.

1. "Father Absence + Involvement Statistics," National Fatherhood Initiative,
   accessed April 4, 2019, https://www.fatherhood.org/fatherhood-data-statistics.

Reflect

In what ways is this week's study exposing the wounds and regrets from your dad or parents?

What promises of God have you learned this week that can heal those wounds?

Take a moment to meditate on the ways God desires to relate to you (see day 2).

Remember to memorize the verse you selected in day 3.

Connect

We've tackled some big topics this week, but God didn't design us to deal with difficulty alone. Please consider sharing with a trusted friend, mentor, or pastor some of the emotions, experiences, and truths you've explored this week.

Intentionally communicate a word of thanksgiving and encouragement to your dad: a card, an email, a text, a phone call, or a face-to-face word of encouragement.

If you've lost your dad to death, consider journaling your gratitude and admiration for him, addressing him directly as if you were writing a letter to him.

If your relationship with your dad is difficult or complicated, consider journaling the hurts and regrets you've experienced because of him, as well as truths you're learning in God's Word. Address him directly as if you were writing a letter to him. Keep your notes in a notebook or a file for now. We'll come back to this activity later in the study.

Your New Family Tree

Start

Welcome to session four!

If you could be related to any person past or present, whom would you choose? Why?

Last week we began unearthing some heavy topics and mining some deep truths. We learned that we need to deal with the circumstances surrounding our relationship with our earthly dad and to embrace the love of our Heavenly Father. And we saw that through Jesus, God wants not only to love us but also to heal us.

What changes when you accept the healing Jesus offers for your hurts?

Today we're going to dig even deeper into the new identity God gives us through Jesus. Because Christ hung on the God-forsaken tree of the cross, you're invited to become part of a brand-new family tree. You still have to navigate circumstances with your earthly family, but you can be born into a new family by faith in Jesus.

Have someone read aloud 2 Peter 1:3-4. Then watch Louie's message.

Watch

Use these statements to follow along as you watch the video message.

We want to know who we are, and we want to know where we came from.

> ## His divine power has given us everything we need for a godly life through our knowledge of him who called us by his own glory and goodness. Through these he has given us his very great and precious promises, so that through them you may participate in the divine nature, having escaped the corruption in the world caused by evil desires.
> ### 2 PETER 1:3-4

Everything you got when you were born again spiritually, you got from your perfect Heavenly Father.

You can live your life under the waterfall of a perfect Father's blessing.

Once you're alive in Christ, you can't do anything to write yourself out of the story of God.

Our lives are free when we let God be the One to identify who we are.

Video sessions available at lifeway.com/notforsaken

Discuss

Use the following questions to discuss Louie's message.

What statement or idea stood out to you in the video? Why?

In what ways have you allowed your family tree to determine who you are? How has your family tree positively or negatively influenced you?

In what other ways do people try to find their identity? Have you tried to identify yourself through something or someone other than Jesus?

In his message Louie talked about our new identity in Jesus Christ. He said, "We have a brand-new identity and new family tree, ... and that family tree overrides your earthly family tree. You can't get rid of your old one, but you have the power to override it and become exactly what God designed you to be."

Why is it important to find our primary identity in Jesus?

How does our new identity in Jesus empower us, regardless of our family background?

Louie said you can never be written out of God's family tree. How could you embrace this truth the next time you feel that you don't belong in God's family?

Pray

Close the session with prayer. Remember to complete the following personal studies before the next group session.

Personal Study: Day 1

Promise Made, Promise Kept

Fatherhood is a matter of great importance to God. We see this priority reflected in the connection between the last words of the Old Testament and the first words of the New Testament.

God, the Promise Maker

As the events of the Old Testament came to a close, God's people were stuck in their stubborn, sinful ways. God's love, grace, and leadership were constantly available to them, but they continually chose to go their own way, trying to figure things out in their own wisdom. They had mostly left behind their idols by this point, but they weren't honoring the ways of God or trusting in His faithful character.

Although the spiritual condition of God's people was grossly flawed, God still had a redemptive plan. In spite of their rebellion, God still loved His people and wanted the best for them. But apparently, He had had enough for a while, because He seemingly remained silent for four hundred years. But look at the last two verses in the Old Testament, the last words recorded before God went silent.

READ MALACHI 4:5-6.

What do these verses teach about God's heart for fatherhood?

Why is it significant that these were God's last words recorded
before a long period of silence?

Those last words of God contain a warning, a clear indication that a day of justice was
coming when all wrong would be made right. But they also contain a promise—that
in the coming days God would seek to make right the relationship between fathers and
their children. God wanted to restore what had gone wrong between dads and their
sons and daughters. He wanted to reconnect the hearts of fathers to their children
and to reposition children under the waterfall of their fathers' blessing.

In a broader sense God was seeking to reconnect future people with the promises He
had given long ago. Yet he wanted to do this in the context of the relationship between
fathers and their children. Once again we see that fatherhood matters to God.

How should God's concern about paternal relationships affect
your concern about your relationship with your dad?

God, the Promise Keeper

Throughout history God has made promises to His people. He promised to lead them,
to provide for them, to defend them, to rescue them, and to save them. He promised
to love them and never forsake them, even though His people often failed to love Him
and often turned away from Him. God is the great Promise Maker.

READ JOSHUA 23:14 AND PSALM 145:13.

According to these verses, God isn't just the Promise Maker.

He's also the Promise _____.

What promises has God kept to you?

After four hundred years the lingering silence of heaven was broken by the cry of a baby in Bethlehem. That's what God had to say next. To a group of surprised shepherds on a Judean hillside, the angel of the Lord said:

Today in the town of David a Savior has been born to you; he is the Messiah, the Lord.

LUKE 2:11

Actually, a few angel visits had taken place in the months leading up to Jesus' birth. The angel Gabriel appeared to a man named Zechariah, promising the birth of John the Baptist. The angel told Zechariah that his son, John, would have a favored role in God's story. John was going to prepare the way for Jesus by calling people to change their ways and turn to the Lord. John was also going to do something else.

READ LUKE 1:16-17.

Compare this verse to Malachi 4:5-6. What promise was being kept in Luke 1:16-17?

Through John, God was fulfilling the last words of the Old Testament. The last words of the Old Testament and the first words of the New Testament are deeply connected. Between them is a long pause for emphasis.

In the first chapter of the New Testament, God was keeping His promise by preparing a way for the hearts of fathers to change. Making a way to restore the relationship between fathers and children. Making a way for your heart to change. Making a way to bring healing between you and your earthly dad. Why? Because fatherhood matters to God. It matters so much because ultimately, He's making a way to bring healing between you and your Heavenly Father.

Before beginning this Bible study, how much did you desire healing between you and your earthly father?

1	2	3	4	5	6	7	8	9	10
Not at all				Maybe a little					A lot

After reading today's study, how much do you desire healing between you and your earthly father?

1	2	3	4	5	6	7	8	9	10
Not at all				Maybe a little					A lot

What truths are driving you toward change?

What roadblocks are keeping you from change?

Malachi's prophetic words came true when Jesus came to earth as God in human flesh. Jesus didn't come just to do some good works and heal diseases. He wasn't on earth just to walk on water and raise His buddy Lazarus from the dead. Jesus came to die, to do what no other person ever born could do. Born of a virgin and without sin, Jesus lived in obedience to the Father so that He could exchange His innocent life for yours. In doing so, He would cancel your debt of sin and death and would offer you the gift of never-ending life.

The Bible teaches us that Jesus is the ultimate promise kept by the great Promise Keeper, for in Jesus all of God's promises find their yes (see 2 Cor. 1:20). God promised to turn the hearts of fathers toward their children and the hearts of children toward their fathers. And He was going to do it through the work of His Son.

What promises of God will you trust in this week?

Why should God's faithfulness to you encourage your faithfulness to Him?

Prayer

Father, I admit that I don't always keep my promises. But I'm thankful that You always keep Yours. Thank You for making a way for fathers and children to be drawn to each other through Your Son.

Personal Study: Day 2

The Tale of Two Trees

One night on a college retreat with my church, the Spirit of God opened my eyes to see the cross of Christ as I had never seen it before. Charles Stanley was teaching on abiding in Christ from John's Gospel. Everything was pretty normal until the response time, when he prayed over the group at the end of his message. Suddenly all extraneous thoughts vanished, and all I could see in my mind was Jesus hanging on the cross. I didn't visibly see the cross, and I don't know what Jesus physically looked like hanging there. Nevertheless, I saw an image of Jesus on the cross, bloody and battered, a ring of thorns pressed into His head and agony on His face.

I was a church kid. I had heard about the cross all my life and believed in its power to save. I had sung about it, read about it, and taught Bible studies on it. But in that moment everything changed. I saw the cross.

What stopped me in my mental tracks was the realization that it was my cross. Jesus was hanging on a cross I should have been on. It was my sin, my guilt, my wrong that had put Him there. And He was enduring all the suffering so that I could go free. That night I hadn't seen it coming, but God had opened the eyes of my heart.

READ 1 PETER 2:24.

Why is the cross central to the Christian life?

God doesn't want you just to know about the cross. He wants you to see it in such a way that it shakes you to the core and awakens you to an eye-opening realization that alters the direction of your life. That's the kind of unveiling He wants to give to you, a revelation that allows you to be changed in an instant.

It's important for us to see that something powerful and gruesome and gutsy happened on the cross. As awful as Jesus' death was for Him, it's the best thing that ever happened to you and me. Once we truly see it, we're free. We see it and confess, "I'm forgiven!"

READ GALATIANS 6:14.

What does it means to boast in the cross?

The first-century Christians had this kind of gaze on the cross of Jesus Christ. They knew the life-changing power the gospel of Jesus had wrought in their lives. They were keenly aware that apart from the cross of Jesus, they were powerless and hopeless in this life. Therefore, they concluded that they had no ability or spiritual work to boast in. The only thing a Christian has to boast in is the cross of Jesus Christ because it's the cross that gives us "everything we need for a godly life" (2 Pet. 1:3).

What are you tempted to boast in instead of the cross?

Never Forsaken

You may be thinking, *I appreciate the fact that Jesus gave His life so that I could be forgiven and have peace with God, but what does that have to do with what happened between me and my dad?* Sometimes we get all tangled up in our family tree, and we fail to see the primacy of the tree that's the cross of Calvary and the vital connection between the two.

Think of it this way. On the cross Jesus willingly took on all the wrong of every one of us. That means God transferred all our wrong—and all of your dad's wrong—onto the blameless life of His Son. Jesus bore the guilt of our sin, and thus He bore the weight of God's wrath that we deserved. Remember what Scripture says about Jesus:

He was pierced for our transgressions, he was crushed for our iniquities.
ISAIAH 53:5

READ MATTHEW 27:32-46.

Is anything about Jesus' crucifixion in this passage new for you? If so, what?

The significance of the baby's birth that broke the silence between the testaments is this: when Jesus chose to die on the cross, He was forsaken by His Father so that you would never have to live a day without a father's blessing. He was forsaken by His Heavenly Father so that you would never need to be forsaken by God. Jesus was forsaken so that you would never have to be forsaken. That's the significance of the title of this Bible study. Thanks to the cross, you're not forsaken.

Jesus accomplished the work on the cross to give you a new family tree. And this new family tree changes everything.

How does the forgiveness you received on the cross motivate and enable you to life with freedom and confidence?

Returning to the Cross

Once your eyes have been opened to the wonder of Jesus' death, you understand that the cross isn't just an important moment in the annals of history; it's the place where you can step into your purpose as you claim God's forgiveness and fatherhood. As your relationship with God is changed, you find that human relationships can also change and by the same means. If you want to go forward toward healing in your relationship with your earthly dad, you must return to the cross of Christ again and again.

As your eyes are opened to see the cross, several key truths about the work of Jesus will help sustain you in the darkest times. I encourage you to meditate on these three truths of the cross.

1. **THE CROSS OF CHRIST REINFORCES THE TRUTH THAT GOD LOVES YOU.** God demonstrated His love for you on the cross in that while you were still a sinner, Jesus died for you (see Rom. 5:8).

2. **THE CROSS OF CHRIST ALLOWS YOU TO KNOW THAT GOD UNDERSTANDS YOUR PAIN.** Your Heavenly Father knows what it's like to watch His Son suffer and die. God isn't indifferent toward your pain. Having been crushed by darkness, He understands what you're feeling.

3. **THE CROSS OF CHRIST PROVES THAT GOD CAN TAKE THE WORST AND BRING SOMETHING GOOD FROM IT.** The innocent Son of God was unjustly condemned and brutally killed. But three days later, by God's power, Jesus was alive again, victorious and free. It's the best thing that ever happened to the human race.

> How could you wield these promises to overcome any family deficits you've experienced?

READ EPHESIANS 4:32.

> In light of the cross, to whom do you need to extend compassion and forgiveness?

The enemy is trying to drive a wedge between you and God by using your relationship with your dad to make you doubt that God's heart is good and His arms are strong. Yet a new understanding and a fresh glimpse of the finished work of the cross can forge a bond between you and your Heavenly Father that can't be broken.

Calvary's tree is always primary over anyone's earthly family tree. On Calvary's tree Jesus made a way for you to join a new family as a forgiven son or daughter of the King. Although He has placed you in your particular family for a reason, through Jesus you're now a part of the best family of all. We'll explore that truth tomorrow.

Prayer

Jesus, thank You for Your willingness to be forsaken by the Father so that I would never have to be forsaken by Him. Help me remember that even if my mother and father forsake me, my Heavenly Father will take me in.

Personal Study: Day 3

Your New Family Tree

One night Shelley and I were making taco salad for dinner, but there was a problem. Soon I was at our nearby grocery store trying to figure out how to select the right avocados we needed to complete our meal. I'll admit it takes a better man than I am to choose an avocado that's ready to eat—not too hard, not too soft. But feeling fairly confident with the four in my shopping basket, I checked out and headed home.

As we cut into the first avocado, halving it to expose its big, round seed, the whole interior was dark gray and mushy. The seed plopped right out on the counter. Yuck! No sweat; we had three more that looked good. We sliced into the second one, and it was worse—rotten and putrid. Somehow, in spite of all my investigative efforts in the produce aisle at the store, I had managed to come home with four worthless avocados. Although they looked fantastic on the outside, these avocados were no good.

A false front is definitely a bummer when the subject is fruits and vegetables. But it can be devastating when worn by someone you trust and love.

Rest assured that God, your perfect Father, doesn't just love you with a love that looks good from a distance. Your perfect Father is good through and through. When you examine His heart, you'll always find His love to be the same. Your Heavenly Father is a good Father, perfect in every season. And He gives good gifts to His children through the new family tree He offers us. These gifts include a new identity, a loving Father, and a new family.

A New Identity

READ JOHN 3:1-8.

The most accurate description of what it means to be spiritually saved is the phrase "born again." But this phrase isn't simply a cliché in Christian culture. It's a revolutionary teaching by Jesus Himself. When a Jewish religious leader asked Jesus how he could enter the kingdom of God, Jesus' answer baffled him:

> ## "How can someone be born when they are old?" Nicodemus asked. "Surely they cannot enter a second time into their mother's womb to be born!"
> JOHN 3:4

Jesus was pointing out the problem of sin (it makes us spiritually dead) and the hope provided by the good news (Jesus had come to give spiritual life). That's why Jesus said, "You must be born again" (v. 7)—born not of the flesh but of the Spirit.

We don't get into God's family by being good enough or trying our best. And we aren't left out of His family because we've been bad or because we don't think we deserve His love. God is an equal-opportunity Heavenly Father who created each of us in His image and loved us enough to give His Son so that each of us could be born again into brand-new, never-ending life.

Based on Jesus' encounter with Nicodemus, what would you say to someone who states, "I believe if I try to be a good person and do good works, God will welcome me into His family"?

A Loving Father

Although it's true that God confers benefits on us when we come to know Him, such as grace, peace, forgiveness, and power, it's important to see that everything we've received is wrapped up in a someone. The blessing isn't a thing. The blessing is a person. God is the blessing. Our perfect Father is good and loving.

Read the following Scriptures and record the characteristic each of them teaches us about our Heavenly Father.

Psalm 34:8

Isaiah 49:15-16

John 3:16

Romans 8:37:39

Whether you come from a blessed or broken relationship with your dad, in what ways is God a better Father than you could have ever imagined?

God shows you what a great place you have in His heart. Every earthly love will eventually fall short. But God's love is bulletproof and sure, outrageous and inviting, personal and powerful. He will never tire of saying, "I love you."

A New Family

In the new family tree given to us through the cross of Jesus, we receive a new identity, and we now relate to a perfect Heavenly Father. But we receive another aspect of God's family tree. We also receive a new family—the Church.

God's family, the Church, isn't a civic organization to which you pay your dues and volunteer your time. It isn't merely a service you attend a couple of times a year on holidays. And it certainly isn't a beautiful building with stained glass and a towering steeple. Sure, the Church is definitely a place where you might volunteer and serve, and worship services are certainly a part of our life together as Christians. But the Church isn't primarily any one of these entities.

The Church is God's ultimate family, a family into which He adopts us as His children and relates to us as our Heavenly Father. And it's also a family in which we relate to one another as fellow brothers, sisters, mothers, fathers, sons, and daughters of the faith.

Read the following Scriptures and record words that describe the Church's role as our ultimate family.

Matthew 12:46-50

Mark 10:29-31

1 Corinthians 12:25-26

Ephesians 2:19

1 Timothy 5:1-2

Have you ever regarded the Church as your ultimate spiritual family? Why should you?

Whether you come from a stable or dysfunctional family, in what ways can the Church relationally compensate for what your earthly family lacks?

Being a part of God's spiritual family is one of the greatest blessings we can experience on earth. The Scriptures teach us that our relationships in the Church aren't *like* family but *are* family. In God's family we have mothers and fathers in the faith to learn from, brothers and sisters in the faith to lean on, and sons and daughters in the faith to invest in. And we'll be family for all eternity.

If you come from a blessed, stable family, an even greater, more enduring family exists than the one you enjoy on earth. See your family tree in light of God's family tree. If you come from a broken, dysfunctional family, God hasn't left you abandoned. He's inviting you into His spiritual family. There's a branch with your name on it. And there's a host of spiritual relatives waiting to give you a place at their table.

What specific steps could you take to more actively invest in your spiritual family in a local church?

Prayer

Father, You're good, and You give good gifts to Your children. Thank You for adding me to Your family, the Church. Please help me contribute to it and to thrive as a member of my spiritual family.

Reflect

What did you learn this week about how much fatherhood matters to God?

List three truths about the cross that will sustain you in times of trouble.

1.

2.

3.

How can God's family tree overcome any deficiencies in your earthly family tree?

Connect

If you're not active in a local church, intentionally pursue a gospel-preaching church you can commit to.

If you're active in a local church, intentionally connect with other Christians who can serve as mentors or encouragers for you.

The next time you participate in the Lord's Supper with your church family, express gratitude to God for the three truths of the cross in day 2.

The Christian faith is characterized by "Come and see," then "Go and tell." Intentionally plan a time to share with someone else some of the truths from God's Word you've explored in this week's study.

Finding Freedom

Start

Welcome to session five!

Last week we talked a lot about our lineage (or ancestry) and discovered that we come from a variety of family trees. Some are strong and prosperous, others are weak and broken, and many others are somewhere in between. We also learned that God really cares about fatherhood—so much that He promised to turn fathers' hearts to their children and children's hearts to their fathers (see Mal. 4:5-6). He brings about this union through the coming of His own Son, Jesus Christ.

What's the most significant truth God taught you in last week's personal study?

How is God leading you to put that truth into action?

This week we'll wrestle with what's most likely one of the more uncomfortable topics in our study together. But I want to urge you to open your mind and heart, leaning into what God may have for you this next week so that you can fully experience the blessing, power, and freedom Jesus has made available for you through the cross.

Today we turn our attention to the subject of forgiving our dads. What seems difficult, or even impossible, from a human vantage point is made possible through the power of Jesus.

Have someone read aloud Ephesians 4:31-32. Then watch Louie's message.

Watch

Use these statements to follow along as you watch the video message.

Unless we let God reset our heart, our heart can't heal.

The way any of us start down the road to forgiving others is by realizing how God came down the road to forgive us.

> ## Be kind and compassionate to one another, forgiving each other, just as in Christ God forgave you.
> ### EPHESIANS 4:32

We are made in the likeness of God. We are re-created as holy sons and holy daughters, completely forgiven by a perfect Father.

If we have the same power in us at our disposal that raised Jesus from the dead, we certainly have the power to forgive our dad.

Forgiveness doesn't begin for you when your dad receives it. Forgiveness frees you the moment you offer it to your dad.

Video sessions available at lifeway.com/notforsaken

Discuss

Use the following questions to discuss Louie's message.

What's the worst physical injury you've experienced, and how long did it take to fully heal?

In his message Louie said, "Unless we allow God to reset our heart, our heart can't heal. And the way God wants to reset our hearts around the hurts of our dad is to lead us to the miracle point of being able to forgive our dad."

When you hear the phrase "Forgive your dad," what do you immediately think or feel?

Louie pointed out that forgiveness doesn't let your dad off the hook. Instead, you get off the hook of bitterness from the past. What's your response to that idea?

Sometimes we forget that our dads are also sons who may be broken or hurt. How could that reality affect your desire to forgive your dad?

How can you bless your earthly family tree through the gifts you've received from Jesus?

Perhaps you were blessed with a father you don't need to forgive. How can you take the principles Louie taught in this session and apply them to another relationship?

Pray

Close the session with prayer. Remember to complete the following personal studies before the next group session.

Personal Study: Day 1

Receiving Forgiveness

Imagine for a moment that you owed a debt, not a car payment or a student loan but a massive, threatening, suffocating, weighty debt. We're talking about billions and billions of dollars. The pressure you feel from your inability to pay oppressively weighs you down with anxiety day after day. Compounding the stress, no matter how many times you make a payment, the balance never seems to shrink. Under the enormity of the debt, you dissolve into hopelessness and despair because it's too much for anyone on earth to pay.

But then imagine this. Someone calls and tells you great news—news you might have imagined in your wildest dreams but never in your lucid mind. Your debt is gone. But it's not just erased, nor has it been hidden or removed. Your debt has been paid off. A grace-filled, merciful benefactor has written the check to pay your balance in full. You're now debt free!

Believe it or not, that hopeless, burdensome condition describes our lives before we came to Jesus for new life. In the Book of Matthew, Jesus told a parable to illustrate how great our sin debt was before God. The details He provided in this story reveal just how much we have to be thankful for in receiving God's forgiveness. It's crucial to grasp the enormity of our debt of offense against God if we're ever going to have any hope of forgiving our dads of their offenses against us.

READ MATTHEW 18:21-22.

What do you think can be inferred about Peter's motives in asking this question?

The parable Jesus told about unforgiveness started as an answer to a question from one of His disciples. Peter asked a simple question:

Lord, how many times shall I forgive my brother or sister who sins against me? Up to seven times?
MATTHEW 18:21

Peter thought he was being lavishly generous. Religious custom required him to forgive someone of the same mistake only three times. Peter may have thought, *I'll not only meet the forgiveness meter, but I'll also double it and even raise it by one more. I'll forgive my brother not three times but seven times!*

However, Jesus raised the standard even higher than Peter's perceived generosity. Jesus responded with hyperbole: "I tell you, not seven times, but seventy-seven times" (v. 22). Jesus was saying that in God's kingdom there's no forgiveness meter. God's children are to forgive without keeping records.

The Great Magnitude of Your Debt

READ MATTHEW 18:23-27.

What stands out to you the most in these five verses?

In Jesus' parable the servant owed ten thousand talents. A talent was worth about twenty years' worth of wages for an everyday worker. Translated into today's economy, his debt would have been billions of dollars. Jesus used hyperbolic language to illustrate the enormity of the debt you and I owe God due to our sin. This parable points to the magnitude of our sin debt before God.

Record some ways the Bible refers to our spiritual state.

Psalm 14:1-3

Isaiah 64:6

Mark 10:18

Many people attempt to be good in hopes that they can earn favor and approval from God. How do these passages counter that line of reasoning?

Like the servant in Jesus' parable, we have a great debt before God. He's perfectly pure, while we're deeply sinful. In our desperation we might try to plead our case just as the servant did. We come to God the way we might approach a car salesman or the university's business office. We say things like "I'll pay you back" or "Can we work out a payment plan?" Spiritually speaking, we might say, "I'll do some good works and earn my way out of debtor's prison." But the Scriptures tell us that even our righteous deeds are like a polluted garment in the eyes of God (see Isa. 64:6).

How do you work out a payment plan for a debt of billions of dollars while trying to repay it with counterfeit bills? It's absurd. You'll never pay it back. And that's the point Jesus was making.

Why is it beneficial to pause and reflect on your spiritual state apart from Jesus?

The Great Mercy of Your God

Jesus' story didn't end with an enormous debt that could never be paid. And neither does ours. After hearing the servant plead on his knees for patience and mercy, the master released him and forgave the debt. Matthew 18:27 says the master "took pity" on the servant. There appeared to be only two options for the master: imprison the servant forever or forgive the debt. He chose to forgive the debt. Why would he negotiate a payment plan for a debt that he knew was impossible to repay?

Spiritually, however, God offers a third option. He doesn't simply forgive your debt of sin. He actually pays the debt for you. The Bible says:

> You know the grace of our Lord Jesus Christ, that though he was rich, yet for your sake he became poor, so that you through his poverty might become rich.
>
> 2 CORINTHIANS 8:9

Your debt hasn't just been abolished, forgotten, or ignored. It's been paid. Paid in full, every penny. Not by a dollar, not by a talent, not by a credit card. It's been paid by the the blood of Jesus.

READ PSALM 32:1-5.

What do these verses say is true of a person God has forgiven?

According to these verses, we must acknowledge our sin to find forgiveness. Why do we avoid acknowledging our sin?

Why is acknowledging our sin actually freeing?

Before being born again, you had a great debt before God. The magnitude of your debt was great, but the mercy of your God was greater. Through the cross of Jesus, your debt has been paid in full. When you acknowledge your sin to God, His mercy showers on you. This is one of the great promises that comes with your new family tree:

If you, LORD, kept a record of sins,
Lord, who could stand?
But with you there is forgiveness,
so that we can, with
reverence, serve you.
PSALM 130:3-4

Once you experience God's forgiveness, you're in a prime position to extend His forgiveness—even to your dad.

Prayer

Father, I acknowledge that I have a debt of sin before You. Yet I can thank You that Jesus paid my debt in full on the cross. Today I receive the promise of Your blessing through Your forgiveness.

Personal Study: Day 2

Extending Forgiveness

When you hear all this talk about forgiving your dad, your first response might be "There's no way I'm forgiving him. You don't know what my dad did. You don't know how deep the hurt is. My dad doesn't deserve to be forgiven. My dad has never acknowledged his wrong. My dad wouldn't care even if I wanted to forgive him. I'm willing to move on, but to forgive what he did to me—I don't think I can do that."

I get it. It's a big deal to let go of something you've carried for a long time. But in Christ, God wants you to see yourself in a completely new way. God wants to bring you out of a state of mind in which you see yourself as the victim of a dad who was busy being an addict or a workaholic or finding himself. God invites you to adopt a new vision of yourself taking your seat at His royal table. You now have the blessing of a perfect Father, along with the position, the forgiveness, and the power of the Holy Spirit that come with being His child.

How would you describe your attitude toward your father?

If you need to forgive your dad, what's the biggest obstacle to offering him forgiveness?

If your relationship with your dad is healthy and intact, what has contributed to the health of that relationship?

Extending What We've Experienced

Your dad may not want forgiveness and may not even think he needs it. But the power forgiveness can bring to you doesn't come when and if your dad receives it. The power of forgiveness that breaks your chains begins the moment you offer it. The reason is that the issue of forgiveness is ultimately a spiritual matter inside your own heart.

Let's go back to Jesus' parable in Matthew 18 to see that forgiveness is a hallmark of what it means to be God's son or daughter.

READ MATTHEW 18:21-35.

How would you describe the primary offense of the unmerciful servant?

The response of the unmerciful servant was absolutely ludicrous. Once his massive debt was mercifully paid, he approached one of his underlings who owed a debt to him. A denarius was a day's wage for an average worker. The unmerciful servant was owed a hundred of them—about four months' salary. And though this debt wasn't insignificant, it paled in comparison to the debt of which his master had forgiven him. Imagine that someone paid off the twenty-trillion-dollar national debt, while the IRS chased you for the repayment of a one-dollar debt. The contrast is preposterous.

This servant clearly demonstrated that he had been forgiven much but forgave very little. Jesus' principle is simple. Becoming God's son or daughter isn't just about gaining right standing with Him. It's about a change in attitude and behavior toward others as well.

How is God using this parable to soften your heart toward forgiving your dad or someone else who has wronged you?

God has extravagantly forgiven us so that we can extravagantly forgive others. We experience forgiveness so that we can extend it. To further drive home these truths, the parable of the unmerciful servant shows us three reasons we should consistently forgive others of the wrongs they inflict on us.

1. WE FORGIVE BECAUSE WE NEED A REMINDER OF RECEIVING GOD'S GRACE. If we don't forgive others willfully and lavishly, we demonstrate that we've forgotten how much God forgave us (see v. 32).

2. WE FORGIVE BECAUSE WE NEED A DEMONSTRATION OF RECEIVING GOD'S GRACE. When we consistently forgive others, we prove that we've indeed experienced God's mercy in our lives. We're extending what we've experienced (see v. 33).

3. WE FORGIVE BECAUSE WE NEED TO HEED THE WARNING OF RECEIVING GOD'S JUDGMENT. If we continually refuse to forgive others, we might show that we've never truly responded to the cross of Jesus and will be subject to God's judgment. Jesus' people forgive because they've been forgiven (see vv. 34-35).

Which of these reasons to forgive challenges you most? Why?

I realize these verses are challenging. They're even tough. But it's not my goal to weigh you down or cause you any more pain than you're already experiencing. Forgiveness isn't easy work, and often the seemingly easier route is to try to lock our disappointment and anger in a closet while we zone out through other things in life. The process of forgiving someone who has deserted us or wronged us is sometimes as painful as the hurt we initially experienced. But the healing is worth the hurt. And though the commands of Scriptures often sound tough, they always prove true.

Power to Forgive

If we refuse to extend forgiveness to our father, that position doesn't punish our dad. Rather, it imprisons us. It anchors us to the negative, while God wants to move us into the fullness of who our Heavenly Father is and who He says we are in Him. It's impossible to fully experience all God has for us while we're holding on to the past with clenched fists.

I gently ask you to consider the following questions.

If you're refusing to forgive your dad or someone else who has hurt you, why might that decision lead to more pain?

How does a refusal to forgive keep us trapped in the past?

Why does refusing to forgive people who have wronged us leave our hearts feeling more unsettled?

If you've willingly extended forgiveness in the past to people who hurt you, how have you experienced God's freedom and blessing?

If your previous answers are mostly negative, please know that God desires to give you the power to forgive. This power causes you not only to see God as a perfect Father but also to extend forgiveness to people who've hurt you most. The Spirit of God within you is that powerful. Remember, the same Spirit who raised Jesus from the dead lives inside you (see Rom. 8:11). If the Spirit of God is powerful enough to resurrect Jesus from the grave, He can definitely empower you to forgive those who've hurt you most.

Your life is no longer dictated by what was done to you. Your life is defined by what Christ has done for you. You aren't a victim but a victor sharing in Christ's victory. You're no longer lying in an ash heap, but you're raised up with Jesus to sit with Him in the heights of heaven (see Eph. 2:6). You're a child of God. And you're free to rise above the past and do for your dad what your Heavenly Father did for you: forgive.

Prayer

Father, I don't want to live in the hurt of the past. I want to live in the power of Your healing. Through the blessing of the forgiveness You've given to me, please grant me grace to forgive those who have wronged me.

Appreciating the Flawless Father

In his book *The God You Can Know,* my mentor, Dan DeHaan, asks you to imagine you're fishing in a small pond, moving around the shore from spot to spot until you've exhausted every inch, only to discover a narrow outflow from the pond. As you follow the little outflow, it opens into an enormous body of water. The little pond was connected to a vast ocean. The body of water you thought you knew in full was only the beginning of a much greater world to be discovered.[1]

The same could be said about my efforts to describe the perfect Father. Trying to exhaust God's character in a few lessons of this study is like trying to fit the ocean into a fishbowl. We've already studied a great deal about who God is and how He relates to us, but today we'll dive a little deeper into God's heart and character as we consider the contrasts between experiences with our earthly dad and those with our perfect Father.

The Perfect Father Is a Provider

One of Jesus' most well-known teachings, the Sermon on the Mount, offers an amazing look at the way God the perfect Father works. Jesus was describing God to His disciples, encouraging them to trust Him in prayer, to go and find out that He doesn't disappoint.

READ MATTHEW 7:7-11.

Jesus asked a couple of rhetorical questions, with obvious answers. The lesson is clear. If human parents, with a propensity toward sin, know what good things to give a child when the child asks, how much more God the perfect Father "provides us with everything for our enjoyment" (1 Tim. 6:17). God is the giver of good gifts.

The key to transforming our thoughts about our father is found in the phrase Jesus used about the stone and the snake. "How much more" (Matt. 7:11) blessing can be found in our Heavenly Father.

How has God shown Himself to be your provider? How does His provision lead you to trust Him?

Jesus was saying, "Look, in the normal course of life, earthly fathers typically know how to meet their children's needs. And on most occasions parents do this. Yet your Heavenly Father will meet your needs and how much more!" The invitation is to see your Heavenly Father as the perfect provider. Remember, He's not the reflection of your earthly dad. He's the perfection of fatherhood.

Because the perfect Father is a provider, He's also able.

The Perfect Father Is Able

It's possible that your earthly dad seemed to forget about you. But not the perfect, faultless Father. In all the ways your dad wasn't there, wasn't able, or didn't see your accomplishments, your Heavenly Father was and did.

When have you felt the personal presence of God?

READ MARK 9:14-29.

Mark related an account about a man whose son was possessed by an evil spirit. Jesus' disciples prayed for the son but couldn't heal him. When Jesus arrived, everyone was arguing about why the boy hadn't been set free. The father implored Jesus, "If you can do anything, take pity on us and help us" (v. 22)—"if you can," meaning "if you're able."

" 'If you can'?" said Jesus. "Everything is possible for one who believes" (v. 23).

The father responded honestly: "I do believe; help me overcome my unbelief!" (v. 24).

The father's words probably express where we all are to one degree or another—somewhere between belief and unbelief. I pray that as you continue this Bible study, your eyes will be opened to see that the perfect Father, who's loving and good, is in control and will provide everything you need. That Father is also able to do all He says He can do.

**Because the perfect Father
is able, He's also present.**

The Perfect Father Is Present

We all long for our earthly fathers to actively participate in our world. Above all, we don't want to be left alone. We want our dad to be there in the important moments. It's part of his blessing. His active participation demonstrates to us that we're important in his world. We matter. Speaking about the perfect Father, the psalmist encouraged us:

**You make known to me the path of life;
you will fill me with joy in your presence,
with eternal pleasures at your right hand.**
PSALM 16:11

Now in Christ we have this promise:

> ## Never will I leave you;
> ## never will I forsake you.
> HEBREWS 13:5

Nowhere in the New Testament do we see the image of God's presence or even a single invitation to seek His presence as we find in the Old Testament. Why? God now lives in believers' hearts through the person of Christ and the Spirit of God. This is how we know we'll never be alone: because Christ lives in us.

How have you felt God's presence with you, even as you work through this study?

Because the perfect Father is always present, He's also a protector.

The Perfect Father Is a Protector

Everyone who has lost a dad to divorce, disinterest, distance, or death has a special place in God's heart. He's committed to you. The psalmist powerfully described His care.

READ PSALM 68:4-6.

What do these verses convey about God's protection?

God is especially in tune with the fatherless. He's especially close to widows, to those who don't have families they can rely on. He's especially compassionate to those who are held captive, either by their own sins or by the sins of others. God, the perfect Father, is the defender of the vulnerable. He abolishes loneliness and breaks the chains of bondage. The God who rides on the clouds is the same God who invites us close to Him, who sings over us and calls us His sons and daughters.

Today God is reaching down with strong arms to lift up any who are fatherless, and He's standing with resolve to defend every widow and orphan. Every time families break, God rides in on the clouds and announces that He wants to be the Father to the fatherless.

When have you turned to God for protection? How did He comfort and assure you?

Are you feeling lonely and without a family? If so, your protector is coming for you right now. His eyes are on you, and His arms are outstretched. He's the perfect Father. The One who's loving and good and in control. The One who will provide everything you need. He's the Father who's able and who's with you and who has been fighting for you every moment of your life. Hear His promise:

Though my father and mother forsake me, the LORD will receive me.
PSALM 27:10

Of the characteristics of our perfect Father we've studied today, which is most meaningful to you?

Prayer

Father, I'm running into Your arms. Teach
me to receive Your provision, depend
on Your power, bask in Your presence,
and take shelter in Your strong arms.

1. Dan DeHaan, *The God You Can Know* (Chicago: Moody, 1982), 28.

Reflect

Did issues with your father surface this past week? If so, what were they?

How do you plan to respond? In what ways do you need to forgive? In what ways do you need to show appreciation?

What specific steps will you take to address your issues with your father?

What's the most significant trait your Heavenly Father perfectly represents, in contrast to your earthly dad?

Provider   Power   Present   Protector

Connect

This week we considered the magnitude of our sin before God and His extravagant grace in paying that debt in full. Take time to record your praise and thanksgiving to God in response to His great mercy for you.

In week three you were encouraged to write your dad a letter by way of journaling. This week we'd like to take it a step further by writing a letter and sharing it.

• Regardless of the status of your relationship with your dad, consider reading your letter to a trusted friend or mentor first. This step will allow you to open up and perhaps dig a little deeper. It will also allow you to gain insight about the tone and grace of your words.

• If you have a good relationship with your dad, write a letter of encouragement and thanksgiving. Either send it to him in the mail or read it to him face-to-face.

• If you have a strained relationship with your dad, take the necessary steps to send your letter to him at a time when you're ready. But remember that this step is more about releasing you from the bondage of the past than about making everything right with one envelope and stamp.

• If you've lost your dad to death or if you've never known him, allow the writing process and sharing with a friend to bring healing to your heart.

Just like Dad!

Start

Welcome to session six, the final week of our study!

What did God teach you during last week's personal study?

If the blessing of having God as our perfect Father was all we received in the relationship, we could end the study now. But God has more in store for us than making us His beloved sons and daughters. A phenomenal responsibility and opportunity come with that blessing: we're invited to model our lives after our Heavenly Father.

In your family, whom do you look or sound like most?

Whether or not we like it, we all look and act just like our mom, dad, or Uncle Billy. We can't do much about that. But today we're going to examine the biblical command to look and act just like God. And we can do something about that.

Have someone read aloud Ephesians 5:1-2. Then watch Louie's message.

Watch

Use these statements to follow along as you watch the video message.

God knows that you have the potential and capacity to be an imitator of God.

> ## The Spirit you received does not make you slaves, so that you live in fear again; rather, the Spirit you received brought about your adoption to sonship. And by him we cry, "Abba, Father."
> ROMANS 8:15

> ## And we know that in all things God works for the good of those who love him, who have been called according to his purpose. For those God foreknew he also predestined to be conformed to the likeness of his Son, that he might be the firstborn among many brothers.
> ROMANS 8:28–29

We model who God is by immersing ourselves in His Word.

The miracle was birth, but birth set us in motion toward maturity.

Video sessions available at lifeway.com/notforsaken

Discuss

Use the following questions to discuss Louie's message.

What statement or idea stood out to you? Why?

On the video Louie said, "The things we're talking about in this study are complicated. What we're doing is unwinding the past and reweaving what God is teaching us. And it's not all going to happen instantaneously. So let's give each other the grace and space to let God do His work in our lives."

The same way a baby grows up physically, a child of God is to mature spiritually. Does that picture help you understand the trajectory of the Christian life? Where would you place yourself in the life cycle of spiritual growth?

We all imitate someone. Who has been most influential in forming your behavior and habits, whether positively or negatively?

The thought of growing up to be like Jesus can be overwhelming. Instead of trying to go from zero to one hundred this year, what did Louie suggest as a better goal?

Louie said in his message, "Not forsaken is a promise. God will never leave you behind. But it's also a doorway. Step into the possibility of growing up to look just like your perfect Heavenly Father."

What are the most life-changing truths you've learned in this study? What specific steps of faith or action is God leading you to take in response?

Pray

Close the session with prayer. Remember to complete the following personal studies to conclude this Bible study.

Children of God

Like you, I have a physical birth certificate, an actual paper copy. I haven't seen it in a while with the advent of online information, but in the old days you needed that piece of paper for all kinds of things, like the day you signed up for Little League baseball and needed to prove your age to determine the team on which you belonged.

Your birth certificate primarily declares that you were in fact born. You didn't mysteriously arrive on planet Earth; rather, at a certain time and in a particular place, you joined the human race. The birth certificate reveals your length and weight at birth. A footprint may be there to link you to the recorded information. Then the two most powerful details about you are listed: the names of your mom and dad. This information records by whom you came to be and says a lot about what you're going to become. In physical terms you don't have much of a choice, given that you're the result of blending your parents' DNA, combining their genes.

What do you know about the circumstances surrounding your physical birth? Where were you born? Are there any interesting stories from the day of your birth?

The most basic biological terms indicate that you received something from your mom and dad, and the result is 100 percent you. That's why, like it or not, you have a strong tendency to grow up to look like, be like, and act like your mom and dad.

Your Spiritual Birth Certificate

Here's a twist. In Christ you've been born twice, so you have a new Father you were created to resemble, and a whole new heritage stream is coming down to you. That means, as we've discussed, that you have two family trees. It also means that you have two birth certificates. One is earthly, one heavenly. On one the date and place you entered this world are recorded. The other records the date and place you put your faith in Jesus as the Savior and Lord of your life. In the case of the latter, that's the moment God brought you from spiritual death to life through your faith in the finished work of Jesus on the cross. Your spiritual birth certificate announces that you were born again, that you're now and forever a son or a daughter of God.

The Scriptures are filled with language describing the truth that faith in Jesus literally gives us a new identity as sons and daughters of God.

Record what each of the following verses says about your identity in Christ.

John 1:12-13

Romans 6:6

Romans 8:11

2 Corinthians 5:17

1 John 3:1

All of this is fantastic news because it means the domino effect of our human DNA, the particular characteristics that constitute the sin nature, can be broken by the power of the life, death, and resurrection of the Son of the living God. The old has passed away. A new life has begun. We're sons and daughters of God. Everything has changed.

What do you remember about your spiritual birthday when you were born again? Who shared the gospel message with you? What led you to embrace it?

How has your life changed since that day?

If you haven't yet received the gift of Christ's gospel and been born again, what's keeping you from making that decision?

Your Spiritual Freedom

Being called a son or a daughter of the Most High God seems like blessing enough. But it gets even better. Jesus' redemptive work means not only that you're adopted as a child of the King but also that you're freed from the bondage of your sin, your past, your regrets, your pain, your abandonment, and any other deficit you've experienced on earth.

READ ROMANS 8:15-17 AND GALATIANS 4:4-7.

What central truths do these passages express about your change in status as a result of the gospel?

If you're no longer a slave to sin but a child of God, how does that reality affect the way you view yourself, especially when you struggle with sin?

Recall the moment when John the Baptist baptized Jesus in the Jordan River. After Jesus came up from the water, a voice was heard from heaven. That voice didn't say, "Hey, everyone, this is My slave! He's going to work really hard and do everything I need Him to do." No, the Father said:

This is my Son, whom I love; with him I am well pleased.
MATTHEW 3:17

Jesus was going to work really hard, and He was going to fulfill all of the plans and purposes of His Father, but the Father wanted to emphasize first and foremost that Jesus was His Son.

It's the same with you. In Christ you're no longer a slave. You're a daughter or a son of the Father. This is the benefit of God's rescue plan. Your identity is that of a loved child. And you're free to follow God and His purpose in your life. You're free to know Him and help others know Him. You're free to set aside your sin and shame and to embrace the full, abundant life Jesus has given you with His nail-scarred hands.

The gospel that gives you a new life frees you from the bondage of the past. Your past hurts no longer have any hold on you. You're free. Through the gospel you can adopt new thoughts and behaviors while overcoming the struggles caused by your parents.

How can the gospel overcome the hurts and struggles of your past?

How does the freedom you've found in Jesus shape the way you live every day?

Prayer

Father, thank You for adopting me as a child of the King. Remind me that I'm free in Christ. Empower me to continually let go of the past for the sake of the future.

Personal Study: Day 2

Imitating God

Do you have a favorite childhood photo? Maybe a picture of you with one or both of your parents? Perhaps it's a picture of you working with your dad or dressing up like your mom. I have them. And when I look at some of those old family photos, I see a lot of family love. But I also see a lot of modeling, when kids look at their fathers and do the things they did. What's happening in that snapshot? All of us are products of our DNA and of the behaviors that were modeled for us.

Do you have any favorite pictures of you with your dad? If so, which ones? What makes them significant to you?

If you don't have any favorite pictures with your dad, that's OK. We're walking through this process slowly, breathing in the truth that God is our perfect Father, constantly shifting our eyes off us and onto Jesus, who reveals God to us. Through Jesus, we can know God. By faith in Christ, we can become the children of God, and as children of God, we receive the Father's blessing. The Father loves us, accepts us, and invites us close to Him.

But remember, there's more than simply receiving the blessing of being beloved sons and daughters of God. At the end of the blessing come the phenomenal responsibility and opportunity to model our lives after our Heavenly Father.

READ EPHESIANS 5:1-2.

What people in your life have been the most consistent models of faith in God?

What specific traits of God have they most clearly demonstrated through their lives?

"Be imitators of God" (v. 1, ESV). Let those words sink in. We're to follow God's example, doing what He does, thinking what He thinks, and caring the way He cares. We're to place our feet in His footsteps. We're to imitate God, our perfect Heavenly Father, the same way children imitate their earthly fathers. We have a responsibility and an opportunity to grow up and look and act like God.

Just like Dad

Maybe you're thinking the idea of imitating God is impossible, but in reality, imitating God isn't out of reach for any of His sons and daughters. The key to imitating God is found in verse 2:

> ### Be imitators of God, as beloved children. And *walk in love, as Christ loved us.*
> EPHESIANS 5:1-2, ESV, EMPHASIS ADDED

Those words "beloved children" are identity words for us, words to rest in and soak ourselves in every day of our lives. We're beloved children! And once we have our new identity in mind, we're to "walk in love, as Christ loved us" (v. 2, ESV). That means we're to imitate God by doing what Jesus did.

Let's look at another New Testament passage that further expounds on the idea of imitating God through our new identity in Jesus. It's in the Book of Colossians, which has similar content to the Book of Ephesians. The apostle Paul wrote each of these books as letters to first-century Christians living in the ancient cities of Colossae and Ephesus.

READ COLOSSIANS 3:1-17.

This passage give us three simple truths for understanding how to imitate our Heavenly Father.

1. WE'RE REMINDED OF OUR IDENTITY IN JESUS (SEE COL. 3:1-4; ALSO SEE EPH. 5:1-2).

What do these verses remind us about our identity in Jesus?

These verses are a powerful reminder of who we are in Jesus. They also underscore the power behind any of our efforts to imitate God. We don't start imitating God by deciding one day we're going to become more spiritual. We don't start imitating God by reading a book of character traits and trying to hammer our habits into new shapes. We start imitating God by knowing we're spiritually born again into a new relationship with God in which we're His beloved children. Because of faith in Jesus, our lives are now "hidden with Christ in God" (Col. 3:3) meaning Jesus is our life (see v. 4). We look to Jesus. Through the power of Christ in us, we seek to imitate God.

How does the power of Christ working in you help you seek your perfect Heavenly Father?

2. WE'RE COMMANDED TO PUT OFF CERTAIN THOUGHTS AND BEHAVIORS (SEE COL. 3:5-11; ALSO SEE EPH. 4:17-24).

What specific attitudes and actions did Paul say to get rid of in order to look like your Heavenly Father?

From the list you made, highlight the attitudes and actions that most frequently plague you.

Take a moment to pray, asking for God's power to put off those characteristics so that you can look more like Him.

3. WE'RE COMMANDED TO PUT ON CERTAIN THOUGHTS AND BEHAVIORS (SEE COL. 3:12-17).

What specific character traits did Paul say to put on in order to look like your Heavenly Father?

From the list you made, highlight the qualities that seem the hardest to grow in your life.

Take a moment to pray, asking God to empower you to put on those patterns so that you can look more like Him. Record your prayer.

The old self, the one we're to put off, is who we were before we started following Jesus. Our old self is bent toward destruction. It loves to be selfish, lustful, rage-filled, and impatient. The old self is guided by our earthly desires, which falsely promise to lead us toward goodness but actually lead us toward evil. Paul was saying, "Do you want to become mature? Then you must realize you have a new identity. You're a beloved child of God now. Throw away your old identity, the one that hurt you, and start living from your new identity, your new self. Your new self is created to imitate God's righteousness and holiness, His justice and compassion." When you put off the old and put on the new, you'll grow up to be just like Dad—your perfect Abba Father.

Prayer

Father, I want to look like You. I want to care about what You care about. I want to love what You love. I want to dislike the values and behaviors You dislike. Please form in me a heart modeled after You.

Personal Study: Day 3

Growing Up Spiritually

Perhaps the invitation of imitating your Heavenly Father doesn't sound appealing to you. Thanks, but you're fine with just the blessing. You're loved. You're accepted. God is involved in your life. So you'll take your new identity as a child of the perfect Father and rest in that identity, content to stay in the blissful innocence of being held like a baby in the Father's arms, never taking responsibility for growing up.

If that's what you're thinking, you're missing out. It's actually in your best interest to desire to develop and mature in Christ. Refusing to grow spiritually would be comparable to going to a barbecue on the beach but wanting to eat baby food—think mashed-up peas—instead of the savory solid food available on the grill. In 1 Corinthians 3 Paul lamented that the believers in Corinth had stayed "mere infants in Christ" (v. 1). He wanted to give them spiritual solid food, but they weren't yet ready for it. He could give them only milk because they were still worldly believers.

Examine your relationship with God. Which of the following terms best describes the stage of your spiritual life?

Newborn   Infant   Toddler   Adolescent   Teenager   Adulthood

Choosing to go deeper in your relationship with God in order to grow in spiritual maturity will be key in confidently moving forward in your relationship with your earthly dad. You see, all along your journey, symptoms of your old self will pop up to accuse you, remind you of your past, tell you you're not good enough, make you question God's goodness, and tempt you to give up. It's nearly impossible for a spiritual infant to face that kind of opposition for a prolonged period of time without spiritual growth. But when you build a solid foundation on the Word of God and depend on the power of Christ inside you, spiritual maturity will give you the strength to endure and overcome obstacles in the Spirit-empowered character of your new self.

READ MATTHEW 7:24-27.

As you conclude this Bible study, what specific storms from the past are you most susceptible to believing or facing?

How does Jesus' illustration encourage you to face these struggles with hope?

Markers of Maturity

Growing up spiritually is often called discipleship. Although discipleship is a relationship with Christ that's lived out in real time, it sometimes helps to picture the process in steps. Let me offer three markers on the road to spiritual maturity, three steps on the pathway of discipleship that we should expect to experience in our lives.

1. WE AWAKEN. When we're growing spiritually, we awaken to who we are and whose we are. The more spiritually mature we get, the more we remind ourselves of the truth of our new identity. We aren't merely followers of God; we have a new essence because of our new relationship with God. He's our perfect Heavenly Father, and we're His beloved children. That's our identity.

Reread key Scriptures about our identity as beloved children of
God that we've explored in this study: Psalm 27:10; John 1:12-13;
Romans 8:15-16; Galatians 4:4-7; 1 John 3:1.

Which of these Scriptures is most meaningful to you and why?

Commit to memorize that passage to reinforce God's truth
in your heart and mind.

2. WE ACCEPT. Another mark of spiritual maturity is accepting the implications
and possibilities of our new genetic makeup. It's one thing to believe in Jesus and to
acknowledge that God is our perfect Heavenly Father and that we're beloved children
of God. It's another thing to truly live out those realities.

READ JAMES 1:19-25.

In the first century some of the early Christians thought faith was an internal matter
of the heart only, something that had little or no effect on their actual way of living. But
James clearly teaches us that the Christian walk requires action and change. God doesn't
adopt us as His children so that we can stay the way we are. If we're truly living in light
of our new identity, our lives will change as we submit to the Holy Spirit's work inside us.

Far too often, even though we're believers, we develop a comfortable tolerance for
our old ways. We walk in fear, shame, or unconfessed sin, and we stay that way. But as
beloved children of God, we have the responsibility to shout, "Enough!" to the old ways
of living. By faith we can claim the light of Christ to guide our pathways. We must not
settle for second-rate living anymore.

Have you developed a tolerance for any particular sins or ideas from your old self? If so, list them.

Now, in big block letters, write over them the word *ENOUGH!*

3. **WE ADOPT.** When we grow in spiritual maturity, we adopt the behavior and character of God. We model our lives after Him. This means we copy Him, emulate Him, shadow Him, echo Him, and mirror Him. Through our intimate relationship with God through Christ, we constantly study the ways He works and moves. Spiritual growth doesn't happen all at once. It happens bit by bit as we persistently walk with Him and adopt His priorities, character, and ways.

READ 1 PETER 1:14-16.

Write this passage in your own words.

The word *holy* may sound like a church word to you, but its definition has enormous implications for you and your imitation of God. To be holy means to be pure, but another aspect of the definition is even more practical. It ultimately means "set apart" or "different." Peter tells us that God's ultimate desire for His children is to be set apart from the world—to look, talk, and act differently than others do. When we're set apart in those ways, we show the world the greatness and holiness of our Heavenly Father.

The Waterfall of Blessing

I don't know what kind of earthly father you had, but I know that God has spanned the gulf between heaven and earth to reach you. And I know if you want a perfect Father, He can be yours. I pray that your eyes are open to see Him as He truly is and that your heart is beating fast, knowing His eyes are on you and His heart is in you. The waterfall of His blessing, full and free, is pouring down goodness and grace today. His spiritual genes have re-created you, and His hand is ready to lead you. You can take your next step as a loved child of the perfect Father.

What's the most meaningful lesson you've learned in this study?

Prayer

Father, I don't know what the future holds, but I know You hold the future. Plant the foundation of my heart in the solid rock of Your Son, Jesus. And though dark clouds may rise and storm winds may blow, I know I'm safe and secure in the strong arms of my Heavenly Father.

Reflect

This week we talked a lot about the importance of imitating God. There are many ways we can grow deeper in our relationship with God. Reading Scripture, praying, fasting, corporate worship, learning from godly mentors, serving others, and sharing our faith are a few. Each of these disciplines is important for a child of God.

Record an action step or a goal for practicing each of the following disciplines.

• **Reading Scripture:**

• **Praying:**

• **Fasting:**

• **Worship:**

• **Learning from godly mentors:**

• **Serving others:**

• **Sharing your faith:**

Which marker of maturity do you need to focus on most? Who could help you grow in that area?

Connect

If you haven't yet done so, connect with another believer to have an honest conversation about what God is doing in your heart. Discuss the following.

Share specific ways you've been challenged through this Bible study and ways God is leading you to respond.

James 5:16 says, "Confess your sins to each other and pray for each other so that you may be healed." Share ways you're tempted to accommodate the thoughts and behaviors of your old way of life.

The person with whom you're sharing may be able to see your strengths and weaknesses more clearly than you can. Ask him or her to share evidence of the new self in your life.

Consider taking the necessary steps toward your dad. Do you need to reconcile? Express gratitude? Hand over your relationship to God? Seek help from a mentor or trusted counselor? Commit to spend more time with your father? What step is next for you? How will you pursue this step?

What one core truth that you learned from this study do you need to take to heart or share with someone else?

Leader Guide

Prepare to Lead

Each session in the leader guide is designed to be torn out so that you, the leader, can keep this front-and-back page with you as you lead the group session.

Watch the session's teaching video and read the group content with the leader guide tear-out in hand to understand how it supplements each section of the group study.

The Big Picture

Use this section to help focus your preparation and leadership during the group session. Take note of the highlighted points.

Cultural versus Biblical

Most people have been taught to think about the issues of fatherhood by our culture, not by the Church. The point of this study is to help participants think biblically about fatherhood, particularly the fatherhood of God. This section should provide assistance in leading from a biblical framework.

Considerations

Everyone has an experience with a father. Many of the people in the group may have experiences that are vastly different from your own. It's good to keep this fact in mind. This section alerts you to some of the assumptions members may bring with them to the group sessions.

Pray

Pray for group members as part of your preparation to lead each session.

Session 1

The Big Picture

All of us have different experiences with our earthly dads. But what unites us is the need that's woven into our souls—the need to be loved, treasured, noticed, and accepted by our fathers. We can't dismiss the craving that's in our hearts for a father's blessing.

God offers us a promise that has the power to change our lives forever. The promise is this. No matter what the circumstances are with our earthly dads, we have a perfect Father in heaven who loves us and wants to pour out His blessing on us.

Cultural versus Biblical

Observing our culture reveals a clear fatherhood crisis. The number of broken homes, single-parent homes, and children in foster care demonstrates a breakdown in the nuclear family. Very flawed definitions of manhood and fatherhood also exist. Some dads want the freedom of casual sex without any of the responsibilities that accompany reproduction. Others want the pride of being "a good dad" in public while abusively oppressing their wives and kids behind closed doors. Still others truly do the best they can, but because of their own hurts they come up short on the dad meter, leaving pain and regret on their kids' pathways to adulthood. Although many great dads in our world lovingly and humbly lead their homes, too many others have left deep wounds and disappointment.

It's important to recognize the many ways the fatherhood crisis has affected your group. But it's equally important to help members realize that the brokenness and pain we experience in our culture doesn't represent the way God designed the family. God can redeem any amount of regret or brokenness we've experienced in our lives. He can and will start writing a better story for our lives.

Considerations

In a group study like this, a range of backgrounds and experiences will be represented—
some who've come from deep dysfunction, some who've come from great blessing, and
others who fall somewhere between the two. Throughout the study, help members
who come from broken backgrounds see that God offers them a blessing they've never
known. Help members who come from blessing understand that God offers them something even greater than they've experienced with their earthly dads.

NOTES

Session 2

The Big Picture

A. W. Tozer said, "What comes into our minds when we think about God is the most important thing about us."[1] And we all tend to move toward the image of God we've created in our minds. It's imperative that we have the right picture of God because accurately knowing God is foundational to understanding how to relate to Him.

As Louie said in his message, "God doesn't want us to know Him officially. God wants us to know Him intimately. God's not inviting you into a handshake relationship. He's inviting you into an embrace—the loving embrace of a perfect Heavenly Father."

Cultural versus Biblical

People have a multitude of different ideas about who God is and what He's like. Some of them are valid. Many of them aren't. In his message Louie talked about some of the erroneous viewpoints people hold about God. Our beliefs about God are shaped by our culture more than we might care to admit. As we progress through this study, it's important to know that God is very knowable. He hasn't left us on our own to define Him through the lens of our culture or our experiences.

The Bible tells us who God is, what He's like, and the ways He relates to us. He's all-powerful, all-knowing, and present everywhere, but God is even more intimate and personal to us. More than any other title, Jesus referred to God as Father. Point your group's attention away from cultural assumptions about God and toward the truth that God desires to relate to them as the perfect Heavenly Father.

Considerations

Our views of God are shaped through a variety of means. Our parents raised some of us us in a biblical church environment. Others' views might have been shaped by professors, friends, media, philosophy, or even harmful life experiences.

Because the members of your group come from diverse backgrounds, guard yourself from assuming that everyone has the same idea of the way to know God. Be careful about using vague generalities like "Everyone knows ..." or "We've all heard ..." Give group members freedom to share their experiences and backgrounds without a fear of being singled out.

Help your group see that we're only beginning our study. Over the course of this study, we're going to slowly gain a deeper awareness of who God is, what He's like, and ways He relates to us. It's OK if it doesn't all make sense yet.

NOTES

1. A. W. Tozer, *The Knowledge of the Holy* (New York: HarperOne, 1961), 1.

Session 3

The Big Picture

The big goal for this study is that when you hear *God,* you'll think *Father* as the over-riding image that comes to mind. Yes, think holy. And mighty. And glorious. But all in the context of Father. God wants to relate to us as our perfect Heavenly Father, and He wants us to relate to Him as dearly loved sons and daughters.

Because our experiences with our earthly dad often inhibit this relational process with God, it's crucial to remember this truth: God isn't the reflection of your earthly father; He's the perfection of your earthly father.

Cultural versus Biblical

Some dads are absent because of divorce, death, distance, or disinterest. Some dads are abusive, and they hurt us. Some dads passively fail to lead us. Others demand too much, causing us to feel that we'll never be good enough. Still others antagonistically exasperate and discourage us throughout life. Of course, good, encouraging dads exist too, but enough distortions of fatherhood are present in our culture to cause lasting damage in our efforts to embrace the fatherhood of God. Each distortion of fatherhood obstructs our view of the perfect Heavenly Father.

That's why the perfection of God has to be our standard of fatherhood. When we know that God is our perfect Father and we live from the identity this awareness gives us, we come alive. Old thought patterns pass away—disappointments, guilt, sorrows, and struggles. Behaviors change for the better. Knowing our identity as children of God transforms our relationship with Him, as well as the way we see other people.

Considerations

One of the biggest hurdles to cross in relating to God as the perfect Heavenly Father is addressing experiences and hurts caused by an imperfect earthly dad. This session will likely begin touching on sensitive issues for some members of your group. As you lead your group through this session, keep in mind the following information.

- People in your group are coming from a wide array of familial backgrounds and experiences—some healthy, some harmful, and everything in between. Refrain from categorically assuming that everyone is hurting, but also be careful not to ignore genuine pain. Ensure your group members that you see the pain but that you also affirm the blessing that's available to them through God, their Father.

- Because of the raw nature of this week's study, some members of your group might be tempted to retreat. Acknowledge the fact that this session might be difficult, but instead of running away from hard truths and powerful emotions, lean into the process of exploring the freedom and power that a right relationship with the perfect Father can bring.

- Continually emphasize that we're on a journey together through this study. With each passing week we'll go deeper and deeper in facing earthly circumstances while embracing heavenly realities.

NOTES

Session 4

The Big Picture

Because of what Jesus has accomplished through His life, death, and resurrection, He literally gives us a new identity through faith in Him. When we receive Him, He gives us the right to be called children of God (see John 1:12-13). When Jesus chose to die on the cross, He was forsaken by His Father so that we would never have to live a day without a Father's blessing. He was forsaken by His Heavenly Father so that we would never need to be forsaken by God. Jesus accomplished His redemptive work on the cross to give us a new family tree. We're now adopted into the family of God. And God's spiritual family overrides both the pain and the blessing of our earthly family. His family is ultimate in priority and blessing.

Cultural versus Biblical

Culturally, our families serve as powerful forces that define much of our identity. Consequently, a dysfunctional home life can evoke feelings of inadequacy, loneliness, or defeat. People from difficult home lives can easily conclude that they're destined for a less-than-desirable life because of past circumstances.

The converse can also be true. People who come from stability and relational blessing might grow up with a strong sense of confidence, connectedness, and victory. They might conclude that they're headed for guaranteed spiritual blessing because of their great home lives.

The cross of Christ speaks truth into both familial circumstances. Regardless of our family backgrounds, the gospel of Jesus ultimately tells us who we are and where we're headed. No amount of dysfunction in our past automatically resigns us to that brokenness in the future. The power of the gospel gives us a responsibility to chart a new course for our lives through Jesus. Likewise, no amount of relational blessing in our rearing guarantees spiritual blessing the future. We're still responsible through Jesus to anchor our identity in a relationship with our Heavenly Father and to live according to His purposes and ways.

Considerations

Help the members of your group understand that being born again not only ensures that we'll go to heaven when we die but also changes our familial circumstances. When we see ourselves as sons and daughters of the ultimate Father, who we are in Him defines everything else in our lives. Our new family tree doesn't remove the complications of our earthly family trees. However, it gives us new eyes through which to see our earthly relationships and a new heart with which to approach our earthly relationships, particularly those with our dads.

NOTES

Session 5

The Big Picture

Because of new life in Jesus, we've been forgiven by God so that we can now forgive others, and this forgiveness includes our dads. In his message Louie said, "Unless we allow God to reset our heart, our heart can't heal. And the way God wants to reset our hearts around the hurts of our dad is to lead us to the miracle point of being able to forgive our dad."

Cultural versus Biblical

Forgiving the wrongs of others is one of the most radical evidences of our life in Christ, especially forgiving deep-seated, monumental wrongs done to us. It goes against social norms and personal feelings. If someone wrongs us, a typical response is to run or lash out. Through self-justification and the affirmation of friends, we convince ourselves that we're right to hold grudges, shut off communication, or end the relationship. We easily become entitled to our feelings of bitterness and resentment. We convince ourselves that this response somehow pays the offender back, but in essence, it only positions us further in emotional debt and despair.

The cross of Christ shows us a better way. Jesus forgave us when we were at our worst—lost in our sin—so that now, through His power, we can forgive others when they've done their worst to us. Forgiveness is a product of our new identity.

Considerations

As you approach this session, be aware that this could possibly be the toughest topic some members of your group could consider. Because you aren't able to completely know the depth of pain that people have experienced from their dads, approach this session with a prayerful dependence on the Holy Spirit for wisdom and discernment in leading your group.

As you facilitate this week's group session, keep in mind these important points about forgiving Dad.

- Forgiving Dad isn't contingent on his desire to be forgiven but on your responsibility as a child of God to forgive others (see Matt. 6:14-15; Eph. 4:31-32).

- Forgiving Dad doesn't free him from responsibility for his actions, but it frees you from the pain of your bitterness and resentment.

- Forgiving Dad isn't about sweeping the past under the rug but about breaking the chains of the past for the sake of your future.

- Forgiving Dad doesn't mean remaining in dangerous circumstances, if that's where you currently are. If you truly believe you aren't safe, tell an authority figure, move to a safe place, and allow God to be the Judge and Avenger of all wrong.

NOTES

Session 6

The Big Picture

The blessings of having God as our Father and of our being His children aren't all there is to the relationship. There's more than simply receiving the blessing of being beloved sons and daughters of God. A phenomenal responsibility and opportunity come with that blessing: we're invited to model our lives after our Heavenly Father.

Cultural versus Biblical

Whether or not we realize it, a lot of modeling takes place in almost every place and life stage in our world. We imitate the way people talk, dress, treat one another, and act. Imitation is written into our nature.

Through the Bible we learn who God is, what He's like, what He says, and how He acts. We get the clearest pictures of Him in the four Gospels of Jesus. Jesus perfectly modeled the ways of God for us. As we read the Scriptures and walk alongside other Christians, we learn more deeply how to imitate God—how to grow up to be just like Dad.

Considerations

During his message Louie said, "The things we're talking about in this study are complicated. What we're doing is unwinding the past and reweaving what God is teaching us. And it's not all going to happen instantaneously. So let's give each other the grace and space to let God do His work in our lives."

We're coming full circle in this session. Remember that the members of your group came from a variety of backgrounds. Some have been able to grasp these truths very easily, while others are still grappling with them. Affirm all members in the progress they've made so far.

The idea of imitating God can be overwhelming. Acknowledge that reality while encouraging your group to keep taking the next step forward in growing in Christ and in becoming like their Heavenly Father.

NOTES